Simple Living, Starting From Scratch

Off the Grid in Oz

This book was written with love for all my family and friends who want to live a Simpler Life, Starting from Scratch.

Thank you for taking the time to pick it up and I hope you find something of interest in these pages.

A special thanks to Steve, for being patient with me while I wrote it.

Remember: Live Simply, Be Happy.

Love Kerri xx

Kerri-Ann E. Price

Please enjoy this beautiful poem, written by Charlie Chaplin. It holds messages to live by.

As I began to love myself I found that anguish and emotional suffering
are only warning signs that I was living against my own truth.
Today, I know, this is "AUTHENTICITY".

As I began to love myself I understood how much it can offend somebody
As I try to force my desires on this person,
even though I knew that time was not right and the person was not ready for it,
and even though this person was me.
Today I call it "RESPECT".

As I began to love myself I stopped craving for a different life,
and I could see that everything that surrounded me was inviting me to grow.
Today I call it "MATURITY".

As I began to love myself I understood that at any circumstance,
I am in the right place at the right time,
and everything happens at the exactly right moment.
So I could be calm.
Today I call it "SELF-CONFIDENCE".

As I began to love myself I quit steeling my own time,
and I stopped designing huge projects for the future.
Today, I only do what brings me joy and happiness, things I love to do
and that make my heart cheer, and I do them in my own way and in my own rhythm.
Today I call it "SIMPLICITY".

As I began to love myself I freed myself of anything that is no good for my health -
food, people, things, situations, and everything that drew me down and away from myself.
At first I called this attitude a healthy egoism.
Today I know it is "LOVE OF ONESELF".

As I began to love myself I quit trying to always be right,
and ever since I was wrong less of the time.
Today I discovered that is "MODESTY".

Now as I began to love myself I refused to go on living in the past and worry about the future.
Now, I only live for the moment, where everything is happening.
Today I live each day, day by day, and I call it "FULFILLMENT".

As I began to love myself I recognized that my mind can disturb me
and it can make me sick.
But as I connected it to my heart, my mind became a valuable ally.
Today I call this connection "WISDOM OF THE HEART".

We no longer need to fear arguments, confrontations or any kind of problems
with ourselves or others.
Even stars collide, and out of their crashing new worlds are born.
Today I know THAT IS "LIFE"!

- Charlie Chaplin

Contents

Page		Page	
4	What Makes A Simple Life?	48	Kombucha
5	Starting from Scratch	50	Healthy Lemonades
7	Bread Making Overview	53	Water Kefir
9	Traditional Bread	56	Honey
12	No Knead Modern Bread	62	Honey in the Garden
14	Pizza Dough	63	Honey Fermentation
15	Sourdough Bread	66	Beeswax
16	Sourdough Bread starter	71	Nuts and Milks
18	Sourdough Bread Recipe	80	Make these from Scratch Too
19	Don't waste the discards	86	Natural Household Cleaning
21	When you don't have time to make bread	88	Homemade Substitutions
26	Fermenting	94	Cornflour Cleaning
27	Fermenting: Easy & Amazing Goodness	95	Household Firelighters
28	Fermented Foods	98	Herbs and Natural Products
29	Brining	99	Herbal Infused Oils
30	Kimchi	100	Make your own Hydrosol
32	Fermenting Fruit	107	Herbal Infused Vinegars
33	From Ferments to Alcohol	109	Make your own Body Care Products
34	Yoghurt	110	Carrier Oils
35	Labneh	112	Healing Balms
37	Milk Kefir	114	Bath Shower and Beauty
38	Kefir Recipes	122	Narnie's Recipes
41	Apple Cider Vinegar	132	Index
45	Fermented Drinks	137	The Last Word
46	Apple Cider Vinegar Shrub		

What makes a simple life?

This question can only be answered by you. Yes that's right. Only you have all the answers, because all of us have different lifestyles, different commitments and different ideologies.

But, for me to answer this question, I would say. …. My idea of a simple life, is doing what I want to do; making the time for those people, jobs and things that bring me pleasure and being as self reliant as I can be, through it all. It's a journey, not a destination and is something that I'm mindful of.

As you would be aware, if you read my first book "Simple Living, Off the Grid in Oz", we live off the grid, which means we are responsible for our own power, water, waste and we also grow a lot of our own food. This was a conscious decision to want to live without reliance on systems outside our gate. A major part of our lifestyle is to create as much as possible from scratch. Whether that means building the structures and infrastructure we required, or making a strawberry pavlova using the strawberries from the garden and the eggs from our chook shed. If we can create it, we will, rather than expecting someone else to do the work for us. It makes for busy time, but we are not often bored, and we can be proud of what we make.

It's easy to say the words "yes, I'm going to live a more simple life" but putting the words into practice, takes a commitment to yourself, that you can achieve the goal and appreciate the time and effort that went into it. Both parts are important.

So where to start? I would suggest starting from scratch, hahahaha. Start from where you are. What is happening in your life that is causing it not to let you relax and enjoy it? If this is something that can be changed, then go ahead and change it. If your home, or your mind space feels cluttered, then go ahead and work on those areas, to remove what isn't serving you well anymore.

I can't go into details about everything you can do, because as I said above this needs to be something you really want to do for you, so I can just talk about what I do. This book and the first one, "Simple Living, Off the Grid in Oz" are filled with so many things that I like to do from scratch. These days, because they become like a second nature to me, I don't even realise just how special it is to have these skills, that I can hopefully pass on to you.

I am a big believer in appreciating what I have and feeling grateful that I have learnt the skills to create my own life. No, it hasn't been all rainbows and lollipops, there have been some major roadblocks that I have had to negotiate, but here I sit, feeling very happy that I can look back and say yes, I have been able to bring my life to a point where simple living has brought me much joy.

So many of my friends and family, who don't live my lifestyle, still look at me like I'm the crazy, witchy woman who would prefer to go to the op shop than to Myers, or would prefer to bake my own cakes than buy them from the bakery, or prefer to create my own natural products for our bodies and our home, than to go the chemist. I'm happy with this. I try not to lecture too often to them about the importance of natural medicine rather than relying on pharmaceuticals, and they tolerate my weirdness, in their eyes, so at the end of the day we still all love each other. We can only be ourselves at the end of the day, right?

Come on let's start your journey, of a Simple Life, Starting from Scratch.

Starting from Scratch

Why create stuff from scratch? And what does that mean anyway? When I refer to making something from 'scratch', I mean making something from the ground up, using the raw ingredients or materials. For example, to build a house, you need to start with the Timber needed to create the framework and add the cladding etc. When you bake a cake you start with the flour, the milk and the eggs and add the other ingredients that add the flavours that you are looking for.

Starting from Scratch, can save you a lot of money. But that's not always the most important reason people prefer to make their own... whatever it is. Sometimes it's about the satisfaction that is gained knowing that you don't have to rely on someone else. And sometimes it's about learning skills that can be passed onto other people. I find it very disappointing, that so many people, have no idea how to create something by using the raw ingredients, but need to rely on someone else to provide the end product for them, and usually at a larger cost.

Another great reason to start from scratch, is that you know exactly what has gone into it. For example I love to create body care products and I like to know that whatever is in them, will not do me or someone I love, any harm. The same goes for the food we eat. I like to know what is in the meals that I serve up. I don't like to eat processed food, because too often, even if the ingredients are listed, they don't actually tell you the full story. Don't get me wrong, we will have the odd take away meal and I do store quite a pantry load of processed foods, because we like to be prepared, but as a general rule, we cook everything from the raw ingredients.

The biggest reason why I love to create from scratch though, is the pure joy and pride I have that I have the knowledge and skills to make something. The end product may not turn out exactly as I had envisioned it, sometimes it's better, and sometimes it's an abysmal failure, but that just means there is room for improvement.

Within this book, I would like to share with you a lot of the different products I like to create from scratch. In my first book "Simple Living, Off the Grid in Oz" I shared a lot of helpful hints, tips and recipes, along with how we live Off the Grid, and within this book, I am going to share a whole lot more, however I will be less focussed on off grid topics and more on creating. It doesn't matter if you are off the grid or not, this book can help you.

I hope you have a try at making the different things and have some fun while you are doing it. So often this knowledge is lost in the world outside the gate, because of people's fast paced lifestyles. I would love to see these skills relearnt if you have forgotten them, and passed along to others, especially the younger generations. At the end of the book, I have included a chapter of a whole bunch of my grandmothers recipes, that she had kept and passed onto me. Some of them came from her mother and grand mother, and I would like to pass them onto my children, so they are here and recorded now, which makes me content.

Let's get started!!!

Live Simple.
Dream Big.
Laugh Lots.
Be Amazing.
Give Love.

Bread Making

Bread Making

Bread is one of those foods that are a staple in most people's cupboards. I have vivid childhood memories of winter school holidays, and after playing outside all morning, would be starving at lunchtime. We would run into the kitchen to find freshly baked bread sandwiches and home made soup, waiting for us. It fuelled us up ready for the afternoon.

Bread is easy to make once you get the hang of it. I love to make it from scratch rather than buying it from the supermarket because it tastes better when it is made with ingredients that you have a say in and with the love of the baker.

There is nothing better than the smell and deliciousness of a loaf of bread straight from the oven. A little tip though. It is better to let it cool down properly before devouring it. But then slather it with some homemade butter and jam. Yummo. Life can't get better than that.

Once you've mastered dough making, you will realise that there are so many awesome and creative ways you can use it.

You could make pizza., savoury rolls, soft dinner rolls or crusty hearty rolls for the kids lunches.

You can make fruit loafs, wholemeal, multi-grain.

I am going to share 4 different types of bread dough recipes. These are basic ones. I am also going to share a few recipes for you to try. These can give you some inspiration to create your own family favourites.

Have fun and don't stress too much about it. If a loaf doesn't turn out perfectly, that's okay because you can turn it into something else. You can dry it and turn it into breadcrumbs. Or how about a Bread and Butter pudding? My stomach is rumbling just with the thought of some of the ways we love to eat bread.

Traditional Bread

I call this type of bread, 'traditional' because it is the way my grandmother made it. It is also, the way I made it the first time.

It is pretty simple and you will make a loaf of bread that is either soft on the outside or crusty. The way to make it crusty is to spray it with water, just before you pop it into the oven and then place a small bowl of water in the oven. Another way to make it crusty is to cook it in a Dutch oven which will do the same thing, as the steam will be trapped.

Once you have mastered the recipe, you will find yourself wanting to experiment. You can try using different flours or add in some flavourings such as herbs and spices. Or you could make a multi grain bread. Really, the list is endless. Get creative and you will come up with your own signature loaf with a recipe that you will want to hand down to your grandchildren.

Basic Bread Recipe (Traditional)

3 cups Bread Flour
1 teaspoon Salt (I like fine sea or rock salt)
2 teaspoons Caster Sugar
2 teaspoons Dried Yeast
390 mils room temperature water.
1 tablespoons Extra Virgin Olive Oil (for covering dough)

Preheat oven to 220c Place a baking tray with water into the bottom of the oven if you want a crusty loaf.

Mix all together well except the oil
Knead for about 20 minutes on a floured surface. (Really work those muscles!)
Cover dough with a bit of olive oil to stop the dough drying out. Place bowl covered with a tea towel in a warm spot and let sit to rise.
After about 40 minutes, the dough will have doubled in size.
Punch the dough down then place it in cooking tin.
Cover it again for a second rise, which will take about an hour.
It will have doubled again.
Make some cuts across the top with a sharp knife.
Spray with water if you want a crusty loaf or don't worry if you want it soft.
Cook for about 25 minutes.
When the bread is taken from pan and tapped on the bottom, it will sound hollow and you know it is ready

Kneading Bread Dough.

Kneading is a big part of the successful loaf of bread. It's really good exercise for your arm and wrist muscles. I like to push down with the heel of my hand, then lift the dough into the middle and then going around clockwise continuing this for at least 20 minutes.

Proving the Dough

Let it rise for about an hour or until it's doubled in size. Punch it down and then shape it or put it into baking tin and let it rise again.

Testing the Dough

When you've had enough of a work out, and want to know if you can stop. Pull some of the dough away and if it stretches without breaking, it is ready.

Give that Dough a Good Punch

After the first rise, punch the dough so it deflates. Then continue with the recipe.

Finished Loaf

Rotate the bread at least once during the cooking process to make sure it is even.

Tap the bottom to test if it is ready.

It will sound hollow when it's ready.

Traditional Bread Making

If you don't like kneading or have trouble with this part of the process, you can use your electric mixer with a dough hook attached, or a food processor fitted with the right blades, to do the work for you.

Kneading the bread well, for at least 20 minutes, will get the glutens working, which in turn will create a better loaf of bread, than skimping on this part of the process.

To check to see if your dough has been kneaded enough, pull some away. If it can stretch about 20cm without breaking it's good to go. If not, then you need to give more.

I always oil the bread before sitting it in a warm cosy spot for it to prove. This helps it to stay moist.

In the winter, I like to prove the bread in a warm place in the kitchen. In the summer I will put it outside in a warm place, but not in the direct sun. Remember to cover it so the bugs don't feast on it before you do.

Sometimes, you will need a bit more water and that's fine. Just add a bit at a time until you are happy with the result.

Adding the yeast to the warm water for a few minutes before adding it to the mix is a great idea.

I like to use a good quality dried yeast and good quality bread flour. Some people will tell you that they use Self Raising Flour or even Plain Flour to make their bread. Personally, I don't feel that these are good options.

Check the bread while it is cooking. Sometimes you will need to rotate it, if it looks like it is cooking on one side more than the other. I usually rotate it once.

Instead of using flour when kneading you can try using olive oil instead.

If you are wanting to make bread rolls then after the first rise, cut the dough into six equal portions and roll into balls. Place them slightly apart on the tray and complete the second proofing rise. Follow the rest of the instructions.

If you make your own butter, try adding the butter milk instead of water.

To make the bread more moist try grating day a old boiled potato into the mix.

If you have whey from home made yoghurt you can use this to substitute 25% of the water.

Try adding some dried herbs to dough. I often like to add dried turmeric, black pepper, thyme, basil and rosemary. It's lovely for a change, especially if served with soup, or making cheese sandwiches.

Try adding sesame seeds to the top of the bread. Spray with water to hold them in place.

Lightly toast some Pumpkin, Sunflower, Flax, Sesame Seeds and add them to the mix.

Instead of using a traditional bread tin for baking, keep the dough in a ball and bake on a baking tray.

Always put a few slices on the dough before going into the oven to stop the bread splitting randomly.

No Knead Modern Bread

I call it my Modern Bread, because this is an incredible way to have fresh bread every day without a lot of effort. Yes, it's true. I love this method. It's a great idea for busy mums and dads who love fresh bread but don't have the time to put into making some daily.

This has to be the simplest method ever, in my opinion. I would recommend everyone have a go at making it.

It literally takes about 10 minutes to make and the dough can sit in the fridge for up to 3 weeks, which is awesome, especially for people who love fresh bread, but don't need a loaf a day.

If it's just me or me and a friend who would like a bit of bread with dinner, then this is perfect. I just take a small ball out of the master, prove it and cook it ready to eat with dinner. Just Perfect!

No Knead Modern Bread Recipe

- 6 cups of good Bread Flour
- 1.5 tablespoons Fine Sea or Rock Salt
- 1 1/2 tablespoons Good Dried Yeast
- 1 tablespoon Caster Sugar
- 3 cups of really really warm water.

You will need a 4.5 or 5 litre container and a permanent spot in the refrigerator for it to sit. Use the container to make the dough in.

Dissolve sugar, salt and yeast in the water. Stir and then let it sit for a few minutes until the yeast has finally dissolved and starts bubbling.

Add the flour and stir and mix with your hands until it changes into a sticky dough. You are finished mixing, when you cannot feel any pockets of flour.

Place the lid loosely on top and let the dough sit at room temperature until it has risen to the top. This my take 1 or 2 hours or less, depending on the room temperature.

Punch it down slightly (if necessary) to fit the lid onto the container. Seal it. Place the container in the fridge for a few hours, or overnight. This dough will keep in the fridge for 3 weeks. The low temperature sends the yeast into a kind of suspended animation. Honestly, the dough only improves with time. The longer you can stand to wait to make a loaf, the better and more flavourful your bread will be.

Whenever the desire for fresh, home-made bread next strikes, take a loaf pan, a cast-iron skillet, a cookie tray, or whatever you want to bake on, and preheat your oven to 450 Fahrenheit (230 Celsius). Grease your pan or place some baking paper on it instead. Oil your hands with some olive oil and pick off a hunk of the dough. (about the size of softball) Form it into a loaf. Greasy hands and a thoroughly chilled dough really help with this. Reseal the container and return the remainder of the dough to the fridge, where it will continue developing its flavour.

Although, there is no need to wait for the formed loaf to reach room temperature, or to proof it. This dough can go from fridge to oven in a minute flat and come out tasting like heaven. However, I do like to let it have some time, say 30 minutes before putting it in the oven.

Slash the top of your loaf with a sharp knife. This step isn't strictly speaking necessary, but it gives a more professional appearance and will stop the top of your loaf will tear itself open randomly as it bakes. Bake your loaf for 30-35 minutes at 450 Fahrenheit (230 Celsius). Place a baking tray with water in the bottom of the oven if you want a crusty loaf.

One batch of dough will make around 3 loaves. My maybe favourite part of this whole recipe is that when you finish your last loaf, you don't have to wash your container. Even if you don't have time to mix a fresh batch of dough, just seal the lid and return the empty container to the fridge. In a week or two when you do want to mix a new dough, the remains of the yeast in the last batch will have deposited a delicious pool of greyish alcohol at the bottom of the container. Just pour your warm water on top of that liquid and follow the recipe as above. Not washing the container is a great way of getting that delicious, three-week-old-refrigerator-dough taste in a dough that is in fact just hours old.

Pizza Dough

While we are on the subject of dough making. I have to include the pizza dough. I love to make pizza's. I mean really, who doesn't love a good pizza. These ones are way healthier than the ones you buy frozen from the supermarket or even the ones you buy fresh from a pizza shop. They are fun to put together, especially if you have lots of different things growing in the garden.

My world famous pizza dough recipe:

500gms good bread flour
1 tsp good yeast
1 tsp caster sugar
300ml water
3 tsp olive oil plus extra olive oil for greasing
15g fine sea salt
1 tablespoon turmeric powder
1 tablespoon black pepper powder
1 tablespoon dried mixed herbs (basil, oregano, thyme)

Mix all the above together and knead well for 20minutes.
Cover with olive oil and then let sit to prove for at least an hour in a warm spot and covered. It should have risen, so now you knead it again for a couple of minutes and place it on the pizza tray. Cover and let it sit for another half an hour.

Our favourite toppings include:

Tomato paste and 1 heaped tablespoon minced garlic spread on base.
Next layer Silver beet leaves, spinach leaves or even lettuce leaves, You can even add some Pak choy or Bok choy, pretty much anything green you have growing.
On top of the green stuff I spread chopped red onion, capsicum, jalapenos, anchovies, Jalapenos, olives and whatever else feels right, on the day.

Over the top of that goes a couple of beaten eggs and then to finish it off a thick layer of a mixture of mozzarella, tasty and Parmesan cheese over the top.

Cook this in a pizza oven or in your regular oven on medium to high for about 30minutes or sometimes a bit longer. Eat it up. yum yum yum yum. Remember this pizza has so many ingredients that are good for you. No need to feel guilty.

Sourdough Bread

Once you've mastered the Traditional Loaf of Bread and the Modern Bread recipe, it's time to have a try at making some sourdough bread.

I mean, really! Everybody wants to tell their friends how clever they are by making this healthier bread version for their families. Why not show off a little bit and try making some of this bread. You can get such a sense of achievement once you have this type under your belt. To be honest, it took me ages to get a good sourdough bread loaf. I didn't give up, though. I kept going until I felt it was all good, or at least good enough. I am not the most patient person, and learning this one is most definitely for the person who is determined to get it right. Hahaha But, I wanted to get it right, because I wanted that crown on my head.

So many people I know have entirely switched over to this type of bread, mainly because they feel it is easier to digest. I personally don't have any issues with normal bread, but like to make sourdough when I know that I am having visitors who are in this group.

It takes a lot longer to create a loaf of bread using this method, which can be part of its charm, when you are feeling like taking things slow. One thing I have noticed is that every loaf has a slightly different taste, so don't be surprised about this when you are on your sourdough journey.

There are a few different processes involved that you will need to learn. Firstly you will need to make a Starter. This is almost like a science experiment and can take at least 5 days for it to be ready. So patience is the name of the game, and attention. It's almost like having a new baby in the house. But once you have it and have looked after it, you will find that it can last years. We use the Starter instead of yeast, so at least that's one less thing to add to your shopping list.

Once you have your Starter then you can move on to making a loaf of bread with it. I use a good Rye flour and a good Bread Flour, sometimes white and sometimes wholemeal. Remember to have fun and stay focussed on the different processes and you will be a Sourdough Bread Master in no time.

Sourdough Bread Starter

All you need is Flour, salt and water. I like to make my starter in a glass jar and named it Stanley. It's a great idea to name your Starter, because as you will find it can be like a spoiled brat or a finicky pet and naming it helps you to relate to it on that level. You will find it can act differently at different times, probably because of the temperature or if you haven't fed it properly.

A couple of good tips.

Never use water from the tap if it is from a town water source. It will have chemicals in it that won't be helpful to the process. Use rainwater, filtered water or distilled water instead. I have found that the water is better added when it is room temperature as well.

Use the best flour you can afford. If you have some Rye flour, then that's great. Rye flour has extra nutrients and the wild yeasts eat it up greedily.

Give your Starter room to grow. It isn't a good idea to give it a tiny little container, because you will likely end up with a mess everywhere when it reaches the top and then oozes out and all over the bench. Better to give it a bigger container from the start.

It will take a week before you can make a loaf of bread and you will feel like you are wasting a lot of the starter because you are throwing it away. But, you don't have to throw it away, you could start a few more and give them to friends. Or you can use it in recipes. I'll give you a couple to try.

If you are like me and won't be making a sourdough loaf all that regularly, you can keep the Starter in the refrigerator and feed it every 5 or 6 days to keep it healthy. When you want to use it from the fridge, you will need to plan ahead. Take it out a day or two before you want to use it. Feed it and let it rest on the bench for at least 12 hours.

Below is a picture of how your starter will react.

Day One

Mix 100grams of Rye Flour with 150grams filtered warm water.

Make sure it is all combined with no lumps.

Cover with a cheesecloth or some paper towel with an elastic band.

Let it is sit in a warm place for 24 hours.

Day Two

Take 75 grams of the Starter and place it in a clean jar
Discard the rest.
Add 50 grams each of Rye flour and bread flour
Add 125 grams of warm filtered water and mix really well.
Let it sit in a warm place for 24 hours

Day Three

Take 75 grams of the Day Two Starter and place it in a clean jar
Discard the rest.
Add 50 grams each of Rye flour and bread flour
Add 125 grams of warm filtered water and mix really well.
Let it sit in a warm place for 24 hours

Day Four, Five and Six

Take 75 grams of the Starter and place it in a clean jar
Discard the rest.
Add 50 grams each of Rye flour and bread flour
Add 125 grams of warm filtered water and mix really well.
Let it sit in a warm place for 12 hours

Repeat this process after 12 hours.

Day Seven and beyond.

Take 50 grams of the Day Two Starter and place it in a clean jar
Discard the rest.
Add 50 grams each of Rye flour and bread flour
Add 100 grams of warm filtered water and mix really well.
Let it sit in a warm place for 12 hours

Repeat this process after 12 hours.

If all has gone well, your Starter is now robust and healthy and ready for use.

When you want a rest from feeding the beast, popping it in the refrigerator will slow it down.

Feed it regularly, say every 5 or 6 days.

Sourdough Bread Recipe

To start making your loaf of bread, you need to make sure the starter is ready to go. If you have been keeping it in the fridge, take it out a day or so before, feed it and let it rest. It's now called Leaven.

To test the Leaven to make sure it is ready to use, take a tablespoon and drop it into some water. If it floats its ready. If it sinks you'll have to wait.

SOURDOUGH BREAD RECIPE

Ingredients
250mls warm filtered water
150 grams Leaven
500 grams Good Bread Flour
1 teaspoon fine sea or rock salt
25 grams Olive Oil

Whisk the water, leaven and olive oil together.

Add the flour and salt and mix with your hands.

Cover the bowl with a tea towel and let the dough rest for about 30 minutes.

Work the dough into a ball and then cover and let it rise to about twice its size in a warm place.
This step can take anywhere from 3 to 12 hours.

You can stretch and fold the dough every couple of hours if you like. This will help the dough to work and will give you a better loaf.

When the dough has finished. Turn onto a floured surface.

Cut it into half to make two loaves or leave it as one.

Take the dough into your hands and shape it into a circle by stretching it down and turning it clockwise.

Place it seam side down into a Dutch Oven which has a light dusting of flour or a sheet of baking paper.

Let it rise again for 1 or 2 hours and it looks puffy.

Preheat Oven to 230c.

Slash the dough, using a sharp knife three times across the top.

Place lid on Dutch Oven and put into oven. Reduce the oven temperature to 200c.

Bake for 20minutes. Remove Lid and bake for further 30 minutes or until bread is deep golden brown.

Crack the oven door open for the next 10 minutes of cooking to allow all the moisture to escape and this will help create a crust.

Cool on wire rack, covered with a tea towel and allow to cool for about an hour before slicing. Enjoy!

Don't Waste the Discards

If you are anything like me, then throwing away half the starter, from making sourdough, everyday can really mess with your No Waste lifestyle. I honestly couldn't stand the thought that I was throwing away all that good starter material. Don't despair, you can use it. Yay.

Here are some recipes to try so that you won't feel wasteful!

Apple Sourdough Pancakes

1 cup stewed apples
1 cup Self Raising Flour
2 eggs
pinch fine Sea or Rock Salt
1 teaspoon dried Cinnamon Powder
1 cup Discarded Sourdough Starter
3/4 cup of milk

Sift dry ingredients together.

Make a well and add Sour Dough Starter and eggs

Start mixing from the inside to the outside incorporating more flour from the sides as you go.

Add stewed apples and keep mixing.

Mix in the milk slowly until the batter is ready.

Add butter to a hot frypan.

Ladle some batter into the frypan.

When bubbles break turn.

Try this recipe with other fruits.

They are delicious served with maple syrup and ice-cream.

I like to also stew the apples with sultanas added instead of sugar.

Let yourself go and get creative.

Chocolate Sourdough Muffins

To make these muffins, you need to prepare the night before.

Mix the following together the night before you want to make the muffins. Let this sit on the bench for at least 12 hours.

1 cup of Sourdough Starter
2 cups Self Raising Flour
1 cup milk (you can use any milk you like, full cream cows milk, goats milk, nut milk or coconut milk)

The next day, preheat oven to 175c and oil a muffin trays.

Mix the following ingredients together

3/4 cup cocoa powder
3/4 cup honey or rice syrup or sugar
1/2 cup coconut oil, or butter, melted
1 Teaspoon Vanilla Extract
1 Teaspoon Fine Sea or Rock Salt
2 eggs

Blend the two mixes together.

Spoon into muffin tray

Bake for 15 to 20 minutes.

They are cooked if a toothpick inserted comes out clean.

Let them sit in the pan for 5 minutes before turning them out onto a cooking rack.

Enjoy!!!

It's really easy to adapt the above recipe to add in whatever you like.

Try some Peppermint Extract instead of Vanilla.

Add some dried Orange Peel.

Add some crushed nuts, especially macadamia, which are my favourites with this.

Have fun and create a signature muffin.

When you don't have time to make bread

Some days you don't have time to make bread the usual way, but would still like something to eat with your soup. Or perhaps you want an English muffin to have with some bacon and eggs. Or maybe you want to make some flat bread.

Here is a really easy way to make these types of foods. They are like the bread when you can't have the bread.

The basic ingredients are Self Raising Flour, Greek Yoghurt and salt. From there you can add in different herbs, spices, vegetables or fruit. This is such an easy recipe and you will find yourself using it time after time, especially on those days when you want it in a hurry.

Basic Recipe

1 cup SR Flour

1 cup Greek Yoghurt (room temperature)

1 good pinch salt.

Mix all together and create a ball, adding more flour if needed.

English Muffins

Make a batch of the basic recipe.

Cut into 6 portions and roll each into a ball.

Pat them down to about 1 cm thick.

Fry them in a pan on low heat with a spray of oil until lightly brown and turn.

Once cooked, turn off heat and let sit for a few minutes before eating.

I like to open these with a fork and add some butter to enjoy with soup or stew.

I also like to split them and toast them before adding a poached or fried egg, tomato and sometimes bacon.

They are also great split, toasted and eaten with jam.

Herbal English Muffins

Make a batch of the basic recipe but add some mixed herbs, dried turmeric, onion and garlic salt instead of plain salt.

Cut into 6 portions and roll each into a ball.

Pat them down to about 1 cm thick.

Fry them in a pan on low heat with a spray of oil until lightly brown and turn.

Once cooked, turn off heat and let sit in frypan with the lid on, for a few minutes before eating.

Sweet Muffins

Make a batch of the basic recipe but add 2 tablespoons of sugar to the flour or 1 tablespoon of either golden syrup or honey

Cut into 6 portions and roll each into a ball.

Pat them down to about 1 cm thick.

Fry them in a pan on low heat with a spray of oil until lightly brown and turn.

Once cooked, turn off heat and let sit in frypan, with lid on for a few minutes before eating.

Pizza Base

Make a batch of the basic recipe.

Pat down to about 1 cm thick.

Add toppings of choice.

Cook in pre warmed oven, set at for about half an hour. Enjoy!!!

Flat Bread

Make a batch of the basic recipe

Cut into 6 portions and roll each into a ball.

Using a rolling pin, roll until about 1/2 cm thick.

Fry them in a pan on low heat with a spray of oil until lightly brown and turn.

Once cooked, place them into a bowl lined with a tea towel to keep warm until all are cooked.

Pasties

Make a batch of the basic and cut into six to eight equal portions, and roll each into a ball.

Flatten out to about 1/2 to 1 cm thick.

Fill with cooked vegetables on one side and then bring edges together after you have moistened with water. Press edges and place on a tray that has been sprayed with olive oil.

Cook in a moderate oven for about half an hour or until lightly browned.

I love to fill with the following:

Cooked cauliflower, broccoli and onion, mixed with a thick cheese sauce. So delicious!!

Easy Scrolls

Make a batch of the basic recipe

Pat it down or roll it to about 1 cm thick.

Spread with Nutella, jam, or stewed fruit etc but not right up to the edges.

Roll carefully and either place the entire roll onto a tray that has been sprayed with olive oil, or cut it into 6 equal portions before placing on a tray.

Cook in a moderate oven for about half an hour or until lightly brown,

Easy Rock Cakes

Make a batch of the basic recipe but add 1/2 cup sultanas or other dried fruit of choice.

Drop dessertspoon fulls of batter onto a greased tray. There will be about 12 cakes.

Cook in a moderate oven for about half an hour or until lightly brown

These aren't super sweet, which suits a lot of people.

Following on from this simple way to make bread like foods with basically using yoghurt and flour, if you substitute the yoghurt for sweet potato or potato you can also make even more variations.

Sweet Potato Muffins

1 cup cooked, mashed sweet potato
1 cup Self Raising flour (sometimes more)
pinch salt.

Mix all together until you have a firm dough.

Let sit for half an hour before the next step.

Create a roll with the dough and then cut it into 6 or 8 even pieces.

Create these into 1/2 inch thick patties and fry them until brown on each side in a frypan that is on low heat.

Herb and Cheese Sweet Potato Muffins

1 cup cooked, mashed sweet potato
1 cup Self Raising flour (sometimes more)
salt, black pepper and herbs you enjoy
1 cup grated cheese

Mix all together until you have a firm dough.

Let sit for half an hour before the next step.

Create a roll with the dough and then cut it into 6 or 8 even pieces.

Create these into 1/2 inch thick patties and fry them until brown on each side in a frypan that is on low heat.

As you can see from these recipes it's easy to create whatever you like with just a few ingredients and some imagination. The point is, these are all very simple and can be made from ingredients that you are likely to have in the fridge and pantry.

I hope you try to play around with the recipes and come up with your own speciality dishes that your friends and family will love .

Mashed Potato Muffins

1 cup cooked, mashed potato
1 cup Self Raising flour (sometimes more)
1 teaspoon salt and 1 teaspoon pepper

Mix all together until you have a firm dough.

Let sit for half an hour before the next step.

Create a roll with the dough and then cut it into 6 or 8 even pieces.

Create these into 1/2 inch thick patties and fry them until brown on each side in a frypan that is on low heat.

This is a good recipe to use up the leftovers

Gnocchi

1 cup cooked, mashed sweet potato
1 cup Self Raising flour (sometimes more)
pinch salt.

Mix all together until you have a firm dough.

Let sit for half an hour before the next step.

Roll into large marble size balls and place in saucepan of boiling water.

Cook for about 15 minutes

Serve with pasta sauce.

A **MANIFESTO** FOR A SIMPLE LIFE

EAT LESS, MOVE MORE
BUY LESS, MAKE MORE
STRESS LESS, LAUGH MORE
FEEL BLESSED, LOVE MORE

find a quiet spot
every day and

breathe

Fermenting

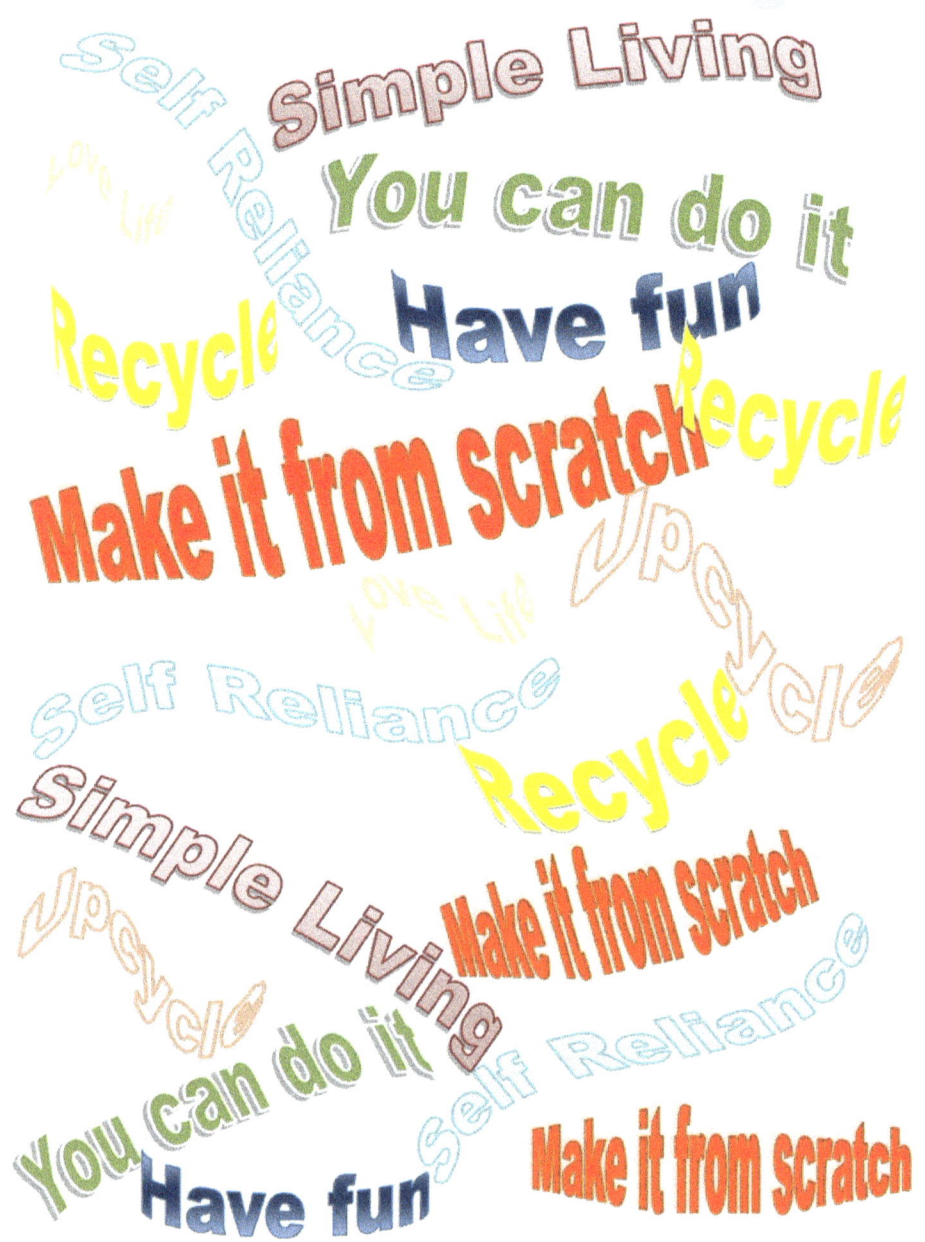

Fermentating Easy and Amazing Goodness

Once you've cottoned on to the fact that fermented foods and drinks are so good for you and then find out just how easy they are to make, you will wonder why you didn't start earlier.

Fermented foods and drinks are full of so many health benefits, especially with their probiotics that your body will just love you for making them a part of your everyday life.

Fermenting is an age old method for preserving foods, which your grandparents may have done for themselves. Mine didn't unfortunately, nor did my parents, so I didn't really start getting into this until I was way into my middle years. I did play around a little bit with it in my 30's but didn't really get into it for another 20 years. Now I love it and it has become a part of my everyday life.

There are just so many amazing ways to create fermented foods and drinks and so many variations that there really is no excuse for you not to find a few that you and your family love and make those.

You are probably already eating fermented foods and don't even realise it. For instance you are probably eating yoghurt or drinking Kombucha tea from the supermarket. That's great, but you can create your own at home at a fraction of the cost. With the added benefit of being creative, using the produce from your own garden and knowing exactly what is included.

Making some beautiful jars of fermented foods and giving them as presents, will no doubt, cause your friends and family to be super proud of you and grateful that you bestowed these healthy gifts upon them.

Don't feel intimidated, it really is simple and fun and doesn't take up too much of your precious time. Your body, your family and your purse will be glad you did.

Fermented Foods

If you haven't heard about how awesome fermented foods are for your body then you have been missing out on some of the most important information that you will ever hear. Well this is my opinion at least. Our guts are home to a lot of bacteria and if there is more bad bacteria than good bacteria then your body will be out of balance. You may find yourself suffering from a lot of different ailments, including inflammations, allergies etc. One great way to help ensure your body can get enough good bacteria to help it balance out the body's systems is to eat a range of fermented foods.

Historically fermented foods were used to preserve foods. They have been around for many many many years. The recipes have been handed down through the generations as have some of the ingredients you need to make them. For example, did you know that man can not create Milk Kefir grains. The ones you use have come from generations upon generations of people passing them around. Amazing when you think of it.

Creating a Jar of Fermented vegetables is so easy and a great way to preserve your garden abundance.

You can ferment in salt, brine (which is salt and water) or you can use whey from your yoghurt, or kefir, or vinegar and sometimes a mixture. I will share with you some of my favourite recipes.

They are all pretty easy. The only thing that I always say though, is, if you see any furry weird mould in the jar, then toss it and chalk that one up to a failure. It rarely happens, but black mould is not good and it is better to just throw it all away and start again. Sometimes you will find mould sitting on the top and you can scoop it out and toss it. But if you are at all suspicious then you are better to be safe than sorry.

If you are new to fermented foods it's a good idea to start off slowly. Try a tablespoon a day for a few days and gradually add more, until your body has created a tolerance for it.

If you buy fermented foods from a shop, remember to only buy what is in the refrigerator and look on the label and do not buy any with added preservatives or if they have been pasteurised. If they were pasteurised then all the good bacteria would have been killed off in the process. For this reason, you are far better off to make your own.

There is no need to sterilise all the equipment and the jars. Just make sure they are clean. The sterilisation can cause the ferments to not work. So there is no purpose to it.

Have fun and play around with recipes to help you find the exact ones that you love. The more you love them, the more you'll make them. The more you make them, the more you'll eat them. The more you eat them the healthier your body will be.

Although, I am sharing a few recipes, there are so many more. Think about making some fermented foods for gifts. Label the jars and decorate them. Always remember to keep them refrigerated and have fun.

Brining

Brining is used when you want to leave the vegetables whole, or in sticks or chunks. Dill pickles are the classic brined ferment. For brining, large pieces of vegetables are packed tightly in a jar, and then a salt water brine is added to cover them. For brined ferments, plan on using about 450g vegetables per 4 cup jar, and about 2 cups of brine. Standard brine strength is 1 teaspoon salt per cup of water, which works well for most vegetables.

Veggies that have a high water content, such as cucumbers or peppers, need a stronger brine - for these use 1.5 to 2 teaspoons salt per cup of water. The maximum amount of salt that can be used is 25%. This solution will not allow any bacteria, good or bad to grow, so if your aim is just to preserve rather than ferment then that's what you will use.

How to make Fermented Vegetables in Brine

Wash and prepare the vegetables as you would before you use them for cooking.

Pack them into a jar and cover with the brine, making sure they are completely submerged.

Poke a knife around to release any air bubbles.

Cover the vegetables with a cabbage leaf to make sure the vegetables cannot get any air.

Place the lid on and put the jar onto a tray to catch any spill overs that may occur during the fermenting phase.

Let sit for between 3 and 7 days, depending on the weather. The warmer it is the quicker the process. The process is complete, when you see no new bubbles forming.

If you let them sit longer, up to 2 weeks before refrigerating, then they will 'cure' which means they will be preserved for a longer period. It really depends on what your goal is. If you have a large harvest and want to preserve the vegetables to use over the following months, curing is a great way to do this.

Place the completed jars in the fridge and eat within a few months.

The vegetables should be still be firm and fresh and taste good. If you notice anything, like mould or a bad odour or they just don't look good, then toss them rather than take any chances that something didn't work.

Kimchi

1/2 head green cabbage or Chinese cabbage, shredded

Plus 1 whole cabbage leaf.

1/2 red onion, diced

1 cup shredded carrots

3 cloves crushed garlic

1/2 teaspoon crushed red pepper (dried)

1 1/2 teaspoons sea salt

1/4 cup whey this is optional, but if you have it use it.

This can be whey from yoghurt or from kefir

Mince garlic
Shred the cabbage or slice with a knife.
Grate carrots or julienne.
Thinly Slice onion.
Mix all the chopped vegetables together in a large bowl.
Add the crushed red pepper and sea salt, and 1/4 cup whey

Let sit covered by a tea towel for about 1/2 an hour, so that the salt can pull out the juices.

Knead the vegetables for a few minutes until you have created quite a lot of juice, enough to cover all in the jar you will be fermenting in.

Spoon vegetables into a clean, sterilised jar and push down as hard as you can and continue to add and push down until you have added all the vegetables.

Add any juices that were created.

Cover the vegetables with the whole cabbage leaf and make sure that all the vegetables are covered.

Place lid on jar and leave to ferment on the kitchen bench for 3-10 days.

"Burp" the jar every 2nd day, to allow extra gasses to escape.

Refrigerate and don't let them sit there eat them up over the next few weeks.

Eat this every day. It's really good for you. But watch out it can be addictive. Hahahaha

You can eat a table spoon of kimchi, if you feel like a little snack or add it as a side dish to your meal.

I like to use the kimchi to make fried rice and pancakes.

You will find it's quite easy to think of ways to use the kimchi. You can create signature blends by using different crunchy type vegetables. Try radishes, kohlrabi, green beans, cucumbers etc.

You can also add a tablespoon of sugar for a sweeter taste. Try adding in some herbs such as dill, cumin, coriander, fennel seed, celery seed, pickling spice, red chili flakes, peppercorns, cloves, juniper berries, fenugreek, bay leaves, or rosemary. The combinations of tastes is endless.

Once you've tried making kimchi, and found how easy it is, you will be making it all the time.

Kimchi Fried Rice

For every cup of cooked rice you will need about 1/2 cup of kimchi.

Make sure the rice is cooked well and dried. Usually day old rice is best.

In a fry pan cook the kimchi in a little olive oil.

Add the rice and stir until heated through.

Serve with a lightly fried egg.

Enjoy.

Kimchi Fritters or Pancakes

1 cup of kimchi,
3 tablespoons of kimchi juice,
2 tablespoons chopped onion,
½ teaspoon sea or rock salt,
½ teaspoon sugar,
½ cup plain flour,
¼ cup of water.

Add all ingredients to a bowl and mix it well with a spoon.

Heat a frypan and add some olive oil or grapeseed oil.

Place tablespoon sized amounts of batter and flatten.

Cook until lightly brown on bottom then flip.

Serve as a side dish or a snack.

These taste good cold as well, so they make good additions for school lunches.

Fermenting Fruit

I have talked a lot about how to ferment vegetables using salt but let's now create some ferments using fruit. There is a big difference in using fruit as a ferment, because already high sugar content, tends to turn the product alcoholic quickly. Now this is great, if that's what you are looking for, but not so great if you want to put it on the kids breakfast.

Any fruit can be fermented. While obviously fresh and organic is the best way to do it, you can also use frozen or even canned fruit.

Fermenting fruit only takes a couple of days and should be eaten within a two weeks from the refrigerator.

I suggest you start with some small batches, to make sure it is consumed relatively quickly. This isn't something that you can keep for months.

Fruit fermentation

Using a 1 litre mason jar, fill to within 2 centimetres from top, with fruit that has been prepared by washing and cutting into about 3centremetre chunks, in the case of say pineapples or pears or halved in the case of say strawberries.

Cover fruit with a brine made by mixing 4 tablespoons honey, 1/4 cup whey, 1/2 teaspoon salt and topped with clean water.

Leave lid off but cover jar with a cloth and sit on the bench for a day or 2. Or close lid and burp every few hours. Stir every now and then.

Lock lid and place in the fridge to slow down the fermentation process.

Consume within 2 weeks.

Fermented Fruit Leather

This is a good way to preserve the fruit from the fermenting process longer, if you don't get around to eating it, or if you would like to create a healthy snack idea.

Drain the liquid from the fruit after the fermenting process has completed. Blend the fruit until smooth. Drain excess liquid by placing in a cloth and squeezing. The liquid is a great probiotic drink, so don't throw it away.

Spread onto a tray, covered with a tea towel and allow to dehydrate overnight. Or use a dehydrator. It is ready when it is smooth and no longer sticky.

From ferments to alcohol

If you want to take your fermenting to another level and create some alcohol, then it is very easy to do. The following is the basic process that can be used when you don't have any special equipment, such as airlocks, which are, by the way, great to use and well worth the investment. But I wanted to share a very simple way for you to try making a small batch to see if you like doing it. There are obviously more ways to create alcohol, such as distilling, but that takes the correct equipment and more know how. This is just a simple way to make a small batch.

Fill a container with the clean, fresh, prepared fruit. Add an equal amount of sugar. (If you used 2 cups of fruit, you need 2 cups of sugar, which means the ratio is 1:1). Add 1/4 teaspoon of yeast or if you are making a really big batch, then add more.

Cover the fruit with slightly cooled, boiled water and stir. Cover container with a cloth and let sit for a few days, up to a week.

Strain fruit out. Place liquid into another clean jar and cover with a cloth and let sit until it has cleared and has the taste you enjoy. This could be a week or two,

Bottle and refrigerate. Enjoy.

In the picture to the right is a special bottle called a carboy. They are glass bottles that have an airlock attached which a great idea to have especially if you would like to start your own hobby of making alcohol.

Try experimenting by adding different flavours, such as cinnamon, or star anise, or Orange Peel.

Let your imagination run amok.

YOGHURT

Yoghurt is incredibly healthy when it's "for real". But it's often hard to find real yoghurt with good milk and live bacteria in the supermarket and when youo do, it's quite expensive. I make my own yoghurt at home and you can too. What a great way to provide your gut with the beneficial bacteria that it needs. That cheap

flavoured, supermarket yoghurt that you are buying isn't real yoghurt it's usually processed to the hilt and will contain additives, food colourings and preservatives! So buying them doesn't give you any of the good things you think you are getting. Either buy a good live yoghurt or make your own. Making your own will save you a lot of money too.

Yoghurt is a fermented milk product. The bacteria used to make yoghurt are known as "yoghurt cultures". Fermentation of lactose by these bacteria produces lactic acid, which acts on milk protein and gives yoghurt its texture and taste.

To make yoghurt at home, for the first time, you will need to buy real, "live" yoghurt, with LIVE bacteria. It is usually more expensive, but as you're going to use it only to make more yoghurt, you'll find that the final cost of your yoghurt will be very low. And it will be the only one you will ever have to buy if you keep on making your own at home.

Next, you need fresh, full-fat milk, that has not been homogenized. It can be Pasteurized, but should not have been homogenized; otherwise, it won't work.

Once you have the milk and the live yoghurt, here is what you do to make yoghurt.

1. Heat 1 litre milk to 70 C in a stainless steel pan. (Just before boiling)
2. Let it cool down a bit until it reaches 40 C.
3. Mix together 3-4 tbsp live yoghurt with 1 cup of the warm milk
4. Put yoghurt mixture back in the pan.
5. Place pan in a warm oven (about 45C), and leave it there, door closed, for 5 to 6 hours, or more. You don't need to keep the oven on, just turn it off.

If you want your yoghurt to be sweet, leave for only 5 hours; if you want it sour, leave for 7 hours. The longer you leave it, the more sour it will get.
6. Place pan in the fridge to cool.
7. When cool, put the yoghurt in clean, glass jars.

Now, I know that you may have read elsewhere that, you need to keep the temperature exact, but that isn't true from my experience.

It takes me literally 5 minutes to heat the milk, preheat oven, and make the yoghurt. Then, I don't worry about it during 6 hours – you may only have to check the temperature and put the oven back on for a minute, to make sure you keep the temperature of 45c during the whole time (especially the first 2-3 hours).

So, that was easy, wasn't it? Enjoy your yoghurt every day and feel proud of yourself for making your own.

Labneh

Labneh is like a soft, fresh, creamy chees. I love making this. It is so easy and versatile.

All you do is place some home made yoghurt (of course you can use bought yoghurt, but make sure it is real yoghurt, set in the pot, because you may as well get the probiotic goodness as well as a yummy snack.

To make it you will need a cheesecloth or use a new chux. Place that into a strainer over a container and spoon the yoghurt on.

Pull the cheesecloth together and tie off so the yoghurt is completely enclosed.

Leave this to sit in the refrigerator overnight to drain and then squeeze out more of the whey.

Marinated Labneh Balls

Make the labneh as above, but add 1/2 teaspoon fine sea or rock salt to the yoghurt before straining.

Make sure you have gotten as much whey out as possible because you want the labneh to be very firm.

Roll up walnut size balls between your palms and place them on a clean cheesecloth to soak up any moisture.

Add the balls to a clean jar.

Add enough olive oil to cover.

Add some dried oregano and zest of 1 lemon and a few chilli flakes.

Store in the fridge.

Sweet Rose Labneh

To 500 grams of yoghurt add 50grams of icing sugar and 3 tablespoons of Rose Water and mix well.

Follow the instructions above for straining.

This is delicious served with berries.

Sweet Chilli Dip

Make some labneh as per the instructions with 1/2 teaspoon of fine sea or rock salt added before straining.

To the labneh add minced garlic and sweet chilli sauce, and chopped chives and mix.

Serve with crackers or corn chips.

Store in the Refrigerator.

Mango Labneh Spread

Blend the meat of a mango and strain as much juice as possible.
Make the labneh with 50 grams of icing sugar added before straining.

Mix equal quantities of the mango and labneh and mix together.
This makes a delicious filling for chocolate sponges. Or spread it on toast.

Store in the refrigerator.

Labneh Mousse

1 1/2 cups plain Labneh
1 1/2 cups light whipping cream
½ tsp vanilla extract,
3 tablespoons honey
2 tsp plain gelatin (powdered)
1 cup water
Whisk together the labneh, honey and vanilla in a bowl, and set aside.
In another small bowl, lightly whisk the gelatin with the water, and set aside for 5 minutes to thicken slightly. Microwave the gelatin for 10 seconds, then mix into the labneh.

Whip the cream into soft peaks, and fold into the labneh mixture until just combined. Spoon into serving glasses and set in the fridge overnight or for at least 2-3 hours

Drizzle with extra honey and top with blueberries or other berries and crushed nuts to serve.

MILK KEFIR

This is such an easy way to get into fermented foods. Milk Kefir grains are like little cauliflowers and they love to multiply and give you a healthy boost to your diet without too many worries. If you have a friend who has kefir, I'm sure they will give you a tablespoon of the grains to start you off, alternatively you can buy them online, readily.

All you need to do, is add a tablespoon of the grains to a glass jar and add a cup of full cream (Organic if you can get it) milk. Cover the jar with a piece of paper towel, secured with an elastic band. Let it sit in a warm place for 24 hours.

What you will find after the day, is a lovely thick white yoghurt looking substance or if it over done then a jar of curds and whey. This isn't a problem, I actually prefer it. You need to strain the curds which are the kefir grains and repeat the process to get the next days supply going.

It's all very simple and I have never had anything go wrong. I like the taste which is slightly tangy and a bit sour. I like to use it as a substitute for yoghurt, but I find it has a few more uses as well. I'll share a few awesome ways to use this beautiful gift of nature, but firstly, did you know that Kefir is good for:

- Adding Probiotics to your daily diet.
- Adding Calcium to help your bones and teeth stay strong
- Makes great smoothies. Just add some fruit and blend.
- Kefir contains tryptophan, which helps relax the mind and body
- Helping your digestive system work better
- A great source of protein without the calories
- Gives you a good dose of Vitamin B.

If you are creating too much kefir and need a break, then all you do is put the grains in the fridge with some milk to cover them. They will keep for a long time like this. When you are ready to make more just start the process again. You can use kefir as a substitute for buttermilk, yoghurt or milk. Remember, though, the probiotics will be killed off when you heat it with cooking, so I prefer to use it mostly for cold dishes.

I like to use kefir in a variety of ways. I like to use it in smoothies with frozen berries and a banana. I've used it to marinate meat, this tenderises it. I've added it to pizza dough and scones and pancakes. I used the curds to make a cream cheese and a savoury labneh. I like to make dips and potato salad and use it as a salad dressing. Really the list is a long one. If you have never tried kefir, you are in for a pleasant surprise. Just another amazing fermented product you can make yourself.

Cashew, Avocado & Kefir Dip

½ cup Cashew Nuts
1 cup kefir curds
2 Avocados
2 tablespoons Lemon Juice|
2 tablespoons Extra Virgin Olive Oil
Fresh or Dried Chilli
Fine Sea Salt & Black Pepper

In a food processor, finely crush the nuts.
Add the avocado meat, lemon juice, oil, chilli and salt and pepper to taste.
Blend until smooth.
Serve and enjoy !

Cucumber Kefir Face Mask

Grate a cucumber into a small strainer over a bowl.
Gently press the grated cucumber into the strainer, collect the juice, and discard the pulp.
Add 2 tablespoons ofkefir to the cucumber juice and mix thoroughly.
Apply to your face and let sit for about 20 minutes.
Gently rinse off and enjoy softer skin.

Kefir Sauerkraut

1 medium Cabbage, cored and shredded
1 tablespoon Caraway seeds
1 tablespoon Fine Sea Salt
4 tablespoons Kefir Whey (if you don't have whey, use an extra tablespoon of salt instead)
Mix all ingredients in a sturdy bowl and pound with a wooden pounder or a meat hammer or just squeeze with your hands (this is actually very soothing and meditative) for about 10 minutes to release juices.
This takes a little work and some patience.
Spoon into a mason jar and using the pounder or meat hammer press down until juices come to the top of the cabbage and cover it.
Cover tightly and keep at room temperature for about 3 days before transferring to cold storage.

Kefir Scones

400g Plain Flour
100g Caster Sugar
1/2 Teaspoon Baking Powder
1/2 Teaspoon Bicarb of Soda
3/4 Teaspoon Fine Sea Salt
175g Soft Butter
250ml Kefir either the full kefir or just the whey.

Preheat oven to 220 degrees C
Sift dry ingredients into a bowl.
Add the soft butter and cut the butter into the dry ingredients using a fork until the mixture resembles dry breadcrumbs.
Add the Kefir and mix.
The dough should be a bit moist, if its too dry add more Kefir, if its too wet add more flour.
Roll half the dough into a ball and flatten on floured surface.
Cut into six equal pieces using a scone cutter.
Repeat with the remaining dough to make 12 scones.
Place on ungreased baking paper/non stick baking tray and bake for 12 minutes.
For a glaze you can brush milk or whey on top and sprinkle with sugar before baking if desired.

Chocolate, Blueberry and Kefir Muffins

1 cup light brown sugar
3 tablespoons soft or melted coconut oil
2 eggs
1 1/2 cups kefir
1 1/2 cups Self Raising flour
1/2 cup semi-sweet chocolate chips
1/2 cup blueberries

Preheat the oven to 200C
Mix the light brown sugar and coconut oil in a large bowl.
Add the eggs, one at a time, and completely incorporate them into the sugar and oil.
Mix in the kefir.
Add the flour, 1/2 cup at a time to prevent loss from mixing.
Stir the blueberries and chocolate chips into the batter until they are fully incorporated.
Spoon into greased muffin tins
Cook 15 –25 minutes
Let the muffins cool for at least 10 minutes when they're out of the oven.

Enjoy!

Kefir Lemonade

Juice from 3 Large Lemons
1/4cup Honey
1/4cup kefir whey
4-6cups Water

Blend all together and refrigerate. Serve with ice and enjoy!

Kefir Cheese

Strain the curds from the whey using a cheesecloth and a strainer over a glass jug. I usually do this overnight in the fridge. Add some Fine Sea Salt, and mix through. Use it like any other soft cheese.

I also like to add some minced garlic and dried herbs, which is delicious. Try adding in some fresh chives too.

Alternatively, if you would like something sweet,

Mango and Banana Smoothie

1/2 cup Frozen Mango Chunks
1 Banana
3/4 cup Kefir
1/3 cup Filtered Water

Blend it all up and enjoy!

Sometimes I like to add 1/2 cup of baby spinach.

APPLE CIDER VINEGAR

Apple cider vinegar is a staple product in my pantry. It is so versatile that I couldn't imagine how we managed to get by without a few bottles handy.

Apple cider vinegar benefits can include improving weight loss, dropping blood pressure and cholesterol levels, stabilizing blood sugar, enhancing skin health, and relieving acid reflux symptoms.

Remember to dilute apple cider vinegar in water, use it in moderation, and pair it with a nutritious diet and healthy lifestyle to maximize your results.

For dull or dry hair, give ACV a try. Making an apple cider vinegar hair rinse prevents dryness, makes it smell great and helps hair stay shiny and lustrous.

The armpits are a great breeding spot for bacteria, which can lead to a worsening of body odour. ACV possesses powerful antibacterial properties and makes an excellent natural deodorant. One of the simplest apple cider vinegar uses is to dab a bit on your fingers and apply under your arms to help neutralize odour and keep you smelling fresh.

If you feel a case of the sniffles coming on, a few tablespoons of ACV may be a useful natural cold remedy to relieve symptoms fast. This is because apple cider vinegar contains beneficial bacteria that can help give your immune system a quick boost, especially when you're feeling under the weather.

Mixing equal parts ACV with water to make an all-natural household cleaner is one of the easiest and most effective apple cider vinegar uses. Thanks to its antibacterial properties, it's perfect for killing off germs and keeping the house spotless.

If your dog or cat can't stop scratching themselves, ditch the chemical-laden flea killers and try this natural remedy instead. Add equal parts water and apple cider vinegar to a spray bottle and apply to the fur once per day until fleas are gone. You can also try making your own homemade bug spray by diluting with water and applying to your skin to fight off pesky insects.

APPLE CIDER VINEGAR

Any sort of apples (core and peel included, no stem)

3 tsp sugar (you can use raw) or more depending on how many apples you are using. (I use a 20 litre container, so I add about 1 cup of sugar)

Enough Fresh, Clean filtered water to make sure apples are submerged.

Instructions

Wash and chop your apples into medium sized pieces (or use the peels and cores of 6-7 small apples after making a pie). Place them in a clean, rinsed and sterilized wide mouth jar.

Mix the sugar with 1 cup of water and pour on top of the apples.

Add more water if needed to cover the apples.

Cover the jar with a cheesecloth and secure it with a band. This keeps nasties away while letting the liquid breathe.

Place the jar in a warm, dark place for 2-3 weeks

Stir it every couple of days with a wooden or plastic spoon.

Strain out the liquid and discard the apple pieces.

Return the liquid to the same jar and cover it again (same cheesecloth).

Return the jar to the same warm, dark place and leave it do its thing for roughly 4 to 6 weeks, stirring with a plastic or wooden spoon every few days or so. (don't stress, if you forget this step)

APPLE CIDER VINEGAR USES

SALAD DRESSING

Try this awesome recipe for Apple Cider Vinegar and Honey Vinaigrette.

Any combination of these ingredients would make a great salad, so feel free to adjust the recipe to your taste! It's perfect for lunch or dinner for two!

Ingredients
3/4 cup extra virgin olive oil
1/4 cup apple cider vinegar
2 tablespoons water
2 tablespoons honey
1 1/2 teaspoons fine sea or rock salt
1/4 teaspoon black pepper

Salad Toppings
2 cups spinach
1 apple, chopped
2 tablespoons walnuts
2 tablespoons raisins or sultanas
1 to 2 ounces of your favourite cheese, diced

Directions

Combine apple cider vinegar, water, honey, salt and pepper in a blender. Drizzle olive oil into blender until combined. Combine dressing & toppings in a bowl; serve.

APPLE CIDER VINEGAR FACIAL TONER

Try this easy facial toner.

    1 part apple cider vinegar
    4 parts water

Mix together in a bowl and apply to skin with a cotton ball or washcloth. Rinse off with warm water after 10 minutes.

APPLE CIDER VINEGAR USES

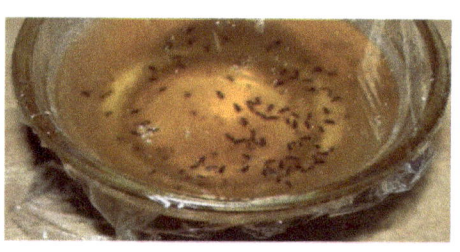

Fruit Fly Trap

Pour a thin layer of apple cider vinegar into a cup and add a drop of dish soap. Set it out on the counter and the fruit flies will fly in and get stuck.

Apple Cider Vinegar Detox Bath

Add 1 cup apple cider vinegar, 2 cups Epsom salts and a few drops of lavender essential oil to bathwater for a relaxing and detoxifying

Apple Cider Vinegar Body Scrub

Mix 2 tablespoons of apple cider vinegar to 1 cup of granulated sugar and 1 tablespoon of honey for a whole-body scrub

Post-Workout Recovery

Fight lactic acid buildup by adding 1 tablespoon to your bottle of water after a workout

Fluffy Rice

Get fluffier rice by adding a splash (about 1 teaspoon) to rice water while cooking. "I LOVE this stuff!! I put a capful into my raw rice before cooking and it's nice

Apple Cider Vinegar Fruit & Veggie Scrub:

Use it to clean fruits and vegetables before eating. Dilute with water in a spray bottle

Fermented Drinks

Fermented drinks are becoming popular again. Once upon a time they were made only in certain cultures, but today, you can buy the ready made ones in the supermarket.

Our guts need the lovely benefits that fermented drinks give. Having a variety will help give you access to different bacteria's they contain.

Everybody has different tastes they prefer, so having the knowledge of how to make a few different fermented drinks is a very handy skill to have.

With all ferments there are a few rules to follow, but once you have the understanding of what is happening with them you will relax and start to experiment with different flavours.

One of the most important factors is the temperature. When the temperature is warm then the ferments will work quicker than if the temperature is very cold. If you are making these in the winter and your house is particularly cold, then you can try wrapping the jars in a tea towel and finding the warmest place for them to work their magic.

Living in the tropics, I have found that some of the ferments will be ready after only 1 day, such as the water kefirs, the kombuchas are usually ready after 2 days. The only one that won't be so worrisome if you are like me and tend to forget them sometimes, are the Shrubs. Once you have prepared a shrub, it can sit with the fruit as long as you like. I have been known to leave it for weeks and sometimes months. The fruit is preserved in the liquid and is edible. The ginger bugs need daily attention, so if you do happen to forget about them, then they will loose their sparkle. However, if you have a lid tightly on them, they could explode because of the gasses that have built up.

Once you have completed the process of making the fermented drinks, pop them in a glass, pop top bottle. This will stop any further fermentation and they taste better cold. Most are drunk straight, however the shrubs are used like cordial. Adding some to a glass and then filling with clean cold water. And unlike the other fermented drinks, shrubs don't need to be refrigerated.

With the scoby from the kombucha, if you want a rest from making it. Place it in some kombucha tea and leave it in the fridge. Feed it weekly.

The ginger bug can be put into the fridge and fed weekly as well, however, it is very easy to start a new batch, so I don't bother keeping it.

The water kefir grains can be dehydrated and stored in the freezer. Or the grains put in the fridge and kept in a small amount of kefir water and fed weekly until ready to use again.

Have fun and experiment with flavours. These healthy drinks are so easy to make. Your body will love you for it.

APPLE CIDER VINEGAR SHRUB

How to make a Shrub

Place your clean fruit in a glass jar and squish down to get it pulpy. Or alternatively, dice it up.

Then add an equal amount of raw honey or sugar. You can add less if it is too sweet.

Then add the same amount again of Apple Cider Vinegar.

That's it. Equal amounts of fruit, honey and apple cider vinegar.

Place it on the kitchen bench for 3 to 5 days. Shaking it when you look at it. Then strain, bottle and refrigerate.

You can drink it like cordial or use it in the gummy bear recipe.

Any fruit can be used. Try some pineapple, orange, lemon, plum, strawberry or whatever fruit is in season. Try a mix of fruits, like plum and raspberry. Try adding some herbs.. I even like to make a mix of apple, lemon, carrot, beetroot and celery. I call this my CABALAC cordial.

Super good for you. Try it. You'll love it!

Plum Shrub

Squash plums into a jar, to release their juices.

Add equal amounts of honey or sugar and apple cider vinegar.

Leave on bench for 3-5 days. Strain and bottle and refrigerate for a few days.

It will then be fine in the cupboard.

Citrus Shrub

Juice a few lemons and oranges or any other citrus fruit you have available.

Juice it. Add equal quantities of honey or sugar and Apple Cider Vinegar.

Let sit on the bench for 3– 5 days.

Refrigerate for a couple of days and then you can leave it in a cupboard.

Mixed Berry Shrub

Squash as many mixed berries that you have
available into a glass jar.

Add equal amounts of honey or sugar and apple cider vinegar.

Leave on bench for 3-5 days. Strain and bottle and refrigerate for a few days.

It will then be fine in the cupboard.

Shrub Remedies

Why not think of using the shrubs as a way to create some herbal remedies.

I like to make something that not only tastes fantastic but is also helping support our bodies when necessary, or just a usual part of our lifestyle.

Cardiovascular Shrub

Remove all the soft fruit from a pomegranate.
Add Blueberries and squash with a fork.
Add a tablespoon dried Hawthorn and Cinnamon.

Add equal amounts of honey or sugar and apple cider vinegar.

Leave on bench for 3-5 days. Strain and bottle and refrigerate for a few days.

Cold and Flu Buster Shrub

Place all the following into a jar
Whole lemon cut into thin slices.
A tablespoon each of dried Mustard Seeds, Black Peppercorns, Garlic, Chilli.

Add equal amounts of honey or sugar and apple cider vinegar.

Leave on bench for 3-5 days. Strain and bottle and refrigerate for a few days.

It will then be fine in the cupboard.

Blood Shrub

Grate Beetroot, Celery and Carrot
Cut whole lemon into little cubes.
Add all to jar.

Add equal amounts of honey or sugar and apple cider vinegar.

Leave on bench for 3-5 days. Strain and bottle and refrigerate for a few days.

It will then be fine in the cupboard.

KOMBUCHA

Kombucha is another favourite in the fermented drinks culture.

Kombucha is made using tea and a scoby. You can buy an organic scoby online or get one from a friend to get you started.

Kombucha is easy to make and is another great way to get the awesome probiotic goodness into your system.

Instructions

For the best brew you will need Filtered Water.

Organic Black and Green Tea Bags (no need to strain loose leaf tea).

Organic raw sugar or white sugar if that's all you have.

Boil 900ml water, then add the sugar and the tea bags or loose tea and allow to brew until cooled down. Remove the tea bags.

Pour into a large mouthed jar and add scoby.

Cover with a cheesecloth and sit on a bench.

Leave it for 5 to 7 days.

Strain, remove the scoby and bottle.

Refrigerate and enjoy when it's cold.

Begin the process again as above, but add some of the kombucha from the previous batch.

I don't mind the taste of the kombucha, cold from the fridge without any further flavourings.

However I do like to flavour it up as well. For example I like to make a tonic which has turmeric and honey for their anti-inflammatory actions.

I also love the benefits of citrus and ginger and it always tastes delicious too. If there are colds or people are feeling run down in the house, I believe that a kombucha flavoured up with ginger and lemon is not only tasty, but all that vitamin C helps our bodies recover quicker.

Try herbs and spices too. Peppermint is great. All you do for the second brew is add a handful of fresh mint leaves.

You can even try some chilli, dried or fresh. Experiment with these drinks and find one that you love.

Anti Inflammatory Kombucha Tonic

700mls kombucha
1 teaspoon Turmeric Powder (it's a good idea to make a teabag if you know how)
1 tablespoon Honey
200mls filtered water
Juice of 3 lemons
1 teaspoon grated ginger

Boil the water add the honey and the tea bag and let brew until cooled to room temperature. Remove the tea bag.

Add the kombucha and lemon juice then pour into a flip top bottle.

Let sit on the bench for a couple of days before refrigerating.

Enloy!

Pineapple Kombucha

200mls Pineapple Juice

700mls Kombucha

Bottle the ingredients and let sit on the bench for 2 or 3 days before refrigerating.

When cool, enjoy!

Flavouring Kombucha

It's easy to flavour your kombucha with anything you like. As you can see from the Pineapple Kombucha I used Pineapple Juice. You can substitute any juice.

If you would like a herby flavour, then add a herbal tea bag to your kombucha for the second brew, or some dried herbs or spices.

Remember a little bit goes a long way, so don't add too much and as you learn what you like you will be making your own signature kombucha flavours.

Have some fun with this and enjoy.

Healthy Lemonades

These are so bubbly and delicious that even the kids will love them. They are simple to make and you could make your signature flavour. I love to experiment with flavours and some of my favourites are Lemberry (Raspberry and Lemon) and Mangapple (Mango and Pineapple).

These healthy drinks are made with a starter called a Ginger Bug, which is just Ginger, Sugar and Water fermented for about a week and then flavoured up with your favourite fruits.

They are probiotic as are all the fermented drinks and foods so they help your gut and because they taste so good are easy to take. Don't you just love it when you find a healthy option that tastes great? I know I do. Have a go at making some yourself.

Ginger Bug

Ingredients

3 tablespoons fresh Grated Ginger
1/2 cup white sugar
2 cups Filtered Water

Add all the ingredients to a jar and stir.

Cover with a cheesecloth or paper towel and secure.

Leave in warm place for 5 days.

Each day, add another 2 tablespoon grated ginger, 2 tablespoon of sugar and 2 tablespoons filtered water and stir.

You will know when the bug is active because there will be bubbles on the top and it will fizz when stirred.

It will also become cloudy and look opaque.

To use the bug, you will need 1/4 cup per litre of whatever lemonade you are making.

To keep the bug alive, keep feeding it as above and add 1/4 cup of filtered water to replace what was removed.

If you aren't going to be needing the Bug and want to rest it. Pop it into the refrigerator and feed it once a week.

NOTES

It may take longer, depending on the temperature.

Don't leave the culture near other cultures because it may cross contaminate and you may end up with something else.

If you see any mould, remove it, but if you see it again, throw out the mix and start again. It's better to be safe than sorry!

Fizzy Herbal Tea

If you love to get more of the awesomeness of herbs into your daily life, then this is something that will make your mouth say thanks.

Whatever herbal tea you like the best can be made into herbal lemonade. Try Lemon Balm, Mint, Hibiscus, Chamomile, Rose Petal etc.

Brew one litre of your herbal tea, stirring in 1/2 cup of sugar. Let it cool down. Strain and add 1/4 cup strained Ginger Bug.

Pour into a pop top glass bottle. Leaving space at the top so the bottle won't explode.

Let it sit on the bench for 3 days and then pop it into the refrigerator for 2 days.

Be careful when you open it as it may fizz over.

Enjoy!

Lemon and Passionfruit Lemonade

This tastes delicious and if you are growing Lemons and Passionfruit then it tastes even better.

Into a blender place the pulp of 2 passionfruit with 1 litre of filtered water and grated peel and juice of 2 lemons. Add 1/2 cup sugar. Blend. Let sit for an hour, then strain.

Add 1/4 cup of Ginger Bug and stir well.

Pour into a pop top glass bottle. Leaving space at the top so the bottle won't explode.

Let it sit on the bench for 3 days and then pop it into the refrigerator for 2 days.

Be careful when you open it as it may fizz over.

Enjoy !

Berry Lemonade

You can use any berries you like. I like to use a mixture of blackberries, strawberries, raspberries and blue berries, but you can just use one if you prefer.

I also like to add the juice of 1 lemon but this is optional too.

170 grams Berries
4 cups filtered water
1/2 cup sugar
Juice of 1 Lemon

1/4 cup strained ginger bug

Place berries, water, lemon juice and water into a saucepan.

Bring the mix to a boil, stirring occasionally, then cover and simmer for 10 minutes.

Cool and strain the mixture.

Add 1/4 cup of Ginger Bug and stir well.

Pour into a pop top glass bottle. Leaving space at the top so the bottle won't explode.

Let it sit on the bench for 3 days and then pop it into the refrigerator for 2 days.

Be careful when you open it as it may fizz over.

Citrus Lemonade

Everybody loves Orange or lemon or lime lemonade. They are all made in the same way, so you can choose which one or which combination you would prefer.

Dissolve 1 cup sugar into 1 cup boiled filtered water and allow to cool.

Add 5 cups cold filtered water and 1 1/4 cups of citrus juice

Add 1/2 cup of Ginger Bug and stir well.

Pour into a pop top glass bottles. Leaving space at the top so the bottle won't explode.

Let it sit on the bench for 3 days and then pop it into the refrigerator for 2 days.

Be careful when you open it as it may fizz over.

Enjoy !

WATER KEFIR

Water Kefir is another easy and healthy way to get the goodness of the probiotics from fermentation.

Water Kefir grains look like little white crystals to me.

Water Kefir is one of the easiest and most forgiving of all the fermented drinks. It only takes a couple of days from start to finish and has a lighter taste than many of the other fermented drinks.

Water Kefir is dairy free, grain free and lots of my vegan friends love it. It also has no caffeine in it as say a kombucha. So it is great for the kids.

Water Kefir is also versatile as it can be used to ferment other types of fluids, such as coconut water or even nut milk.

The grains are quick to multiply so you can easily share with your friends if you find you have too much, or feed them to the chooks. They will love you for this extra special treat.

How to make Water Kefir

This is so simple to make and not many ingredients.

3 1/2 cups of filtered water 1/4 cup sugar (you can also use molasses, but don't use raw honey) 2 tablespoons Water Kefir Grains.

Place everything in a jar and cover with a cheese cloth or chux, or even a paper towel.

Let sit on the bench for a couple of days. If you leave them longer the grains will start to disintegrate.

Strain out the grains and refrigerate in a glass bottle.

You can enjoy the drink like this or you can create a second fermentation and create more flavours.

As with all fermented drinks, creating a drink that you like is part of the fun. There is no right or wrong flavours.

I will share a few of my favourites but these can be adjusted to your particular tastes. Or if you are trying to create different benefits then do some research to find out which herbs, spices, fruits and vegetables will give you the extra help that you are looking for.

The warmer the temperature the faster the fermentation, so keep an eye on them, especially in the summer.

Ginger Lemon

2 cups strained kefir
2 slices of ginger root thinly sliced
1/4 lemon cut into wedges
1/2 tsp honey (optional, but it can create extra fizz)

Follow instructions for Strawberry Mint Kefir

Rose Honey

2 cups strained kefir
1/2 cup fresh or dried fragrant red rose petals
1/2 tsp honey

Follow instructions for Strawberry Mint Kefir

Strawberry Mint Kefir

2 cups strained kefir
3 strawberries, chopped
4 mint leaves chopped

Add all ingredients to a glass mason jar with lid on.

Let sit on bench for a couple of days
Strain and refrigerate.

Keep an eye on it and burp every 12 hours if the gasses are building up. Sometimes the gasses build up so much that explosions happen. It's rare, but worth noting.

Lemon and Lime and Blueberry

2 cups strained kefir
1/4 lemon cut into wedges
1/2 lime cut into wedges
10 blue berries squashed
1/2 tsp honey (optional, but it can create extra fizz)

Follow instructions for Strawberry Mint Kefir

Plum Honey

2 cups strained kefir
2 plums, diced
1/2 tsp honey

Follow instructions for Strawberry Mint Kefir

Being organized isn't about getting rid of everything you own or trying to become a different person, It's about living the way you want to live, *but better...*

- ANDREW MELLEN -

Honey

You can do it

HONEY

In my opinion, Honey is magical. I appreciate it so much and it gets used in our house every day for one thing or another.

We keep bees, so once we harvest the hives, we have enough honey to be able to use it in a variety of ways and not worry too much about the cost. I am very aware that if you don't have access to local raw honey at a discounted cost, at least, then I'm sure you will need to pick and choose what you do with the honey you buy. But I suggest that having a stock of honey in the pantry is an awesome thing to do.

Honey can be used as a sweetener in place of sugar. I like to use it to make strawberry jam because it gives the jam a richer taste. I use honey in my Apple Cider vinegar Shrubs; in some of my vegetable ferments; in baked goods; as a glaze when cooking certain dishes; in my hair rinse and other facial and hair products; as a first aid item; in herbal preparations and a whole lot more.

You can see why we decided that beekeeping was a great money saver for us. Although, it is isn't just for the money saving that we keep the bees. They are just beautiful little creatures that are more like pets. We love to watch them buzzing around, drinking from the bee fountain and pollinating our plants. I would love to see more people take up this hobby and reap all the rewards.

Honey has many amazing qualities. Yes, it is obviously sweet, which is a bonus because it helps encourage the medicine to go down, without all the carry on. I often disguise a herbal remedy in some honey, and no one is the wiser.

Honey in itself is a whole food. It has great nutritional benefits that I'm sure you are aware of.

WE LOVE OUR HONEY !!!!

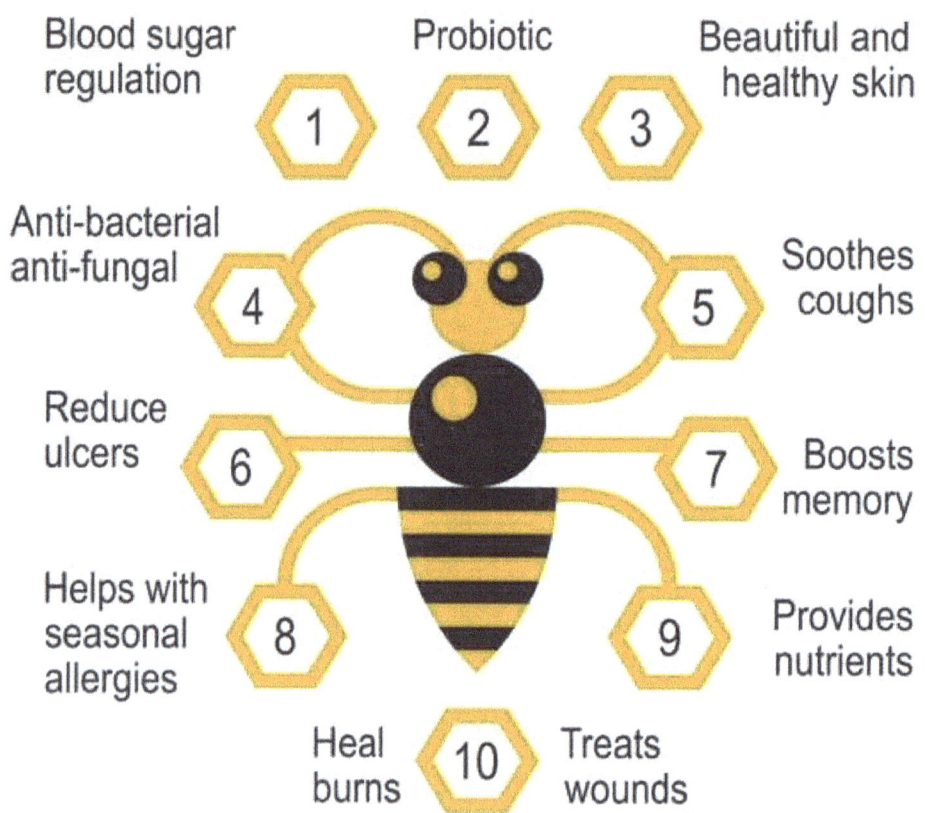

Try some of these ideas for your HONEY

Sleeping Aid

A) 1 teaspoon of honey with a pinch of sea salt before bed can help get a better nights sleep.

B) 1 teaspoon Infused herbal honey (try valerian, passionflower, chamomile, lavender) with a pinch of sea salt before bed

C) A cup of green tea before bed, sweetened with 1 teaspoon of honey or infused herbal honey.

Wound care

Honey disinfects wounds, sores and can be used to treat burns.

Place the honey on a sterile gauze and apply to the cleaned wound. Replace as necessary and obviously see a doctor if required.

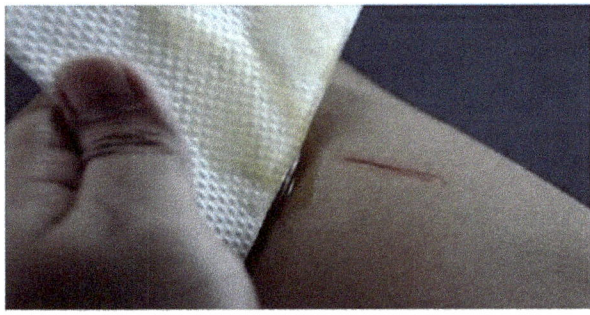

Cough and sore throat reliever

Try a heaped teaspoon of honey.

You can either eat it straight from the spoon or try adding it to some warm water with some lemon juice and sea salt added. Sip as required

Beat those seasonal allergies with honey

Eat some local honey every day, especially through winter, so that your body can build up its own immune system to fight off seasonal allergies.

Try some of these ideas for your HAIR using HONEY

Honey is great for hair, it helps to:

- Restore shine
- improve condition of natural hair
- reduce frizz
- soften hair
- Moisturise dry hair and scalp
- reduce hair breakage

Honey Hair Mask

Mix 1/2 cup honey with 1/4 cup olive oil in a plastic squeezable bottle fitted with a nozzle.

Warm in microwave to blend easily.

Dampen Hair.

Apply Honey mixture, starting at the scalp.

Gently massage.

Place a shower cap onto hair and leave for about 30 minutes, before rinsing out with warm water.

Shampoo and condition as usual.

Honey and Apple Cider Vinegar Hair Rinse

I use this instead of conditioners. It leaves my hair feeling beautiful.

Into a plastic squeezy bottle add 1 tablespoon honey, 1/3 cup apple cider vinegar, 1 teaspoon conditioner, 5 drops each Rosemary, Cedarwood and Lavender Essential oils. Fill with warm water. Shake to combine.

To use: Apply to freshly washed hair. Leave for a minute or so, then rinse out with warm water.

Herbal Honey Pills

If you are looking for a good way to take a herbal remedy, then it is often easy to make some herbal pills.

All you do is mix a a ratio of 2:1 Herbs to Honey. Which means if you use 1 cup of powdered herbs you will need to blend it with 1/2 cup honey.

Once mixed, make some balls using 1/2 teaspoon of the mixture. I like to roll them into powdered marshmallow root, before placing them onto a tray and then covering them with a tea towel. They are then left to dry in a warm place. This may take a few days, or you can use a dehydrator.

Store them in a clean, dry, dark glass jar with an oxygen absorber.

I usually take 1 to 2 pills 2 or 3 times a day. But this will

Please remember to do your own research

and only use safe herbs that you have no allergies to.

Honey Herbal Lozenges (cough drops)

1 teabag (1 tblsp) peppermint tea leaves
1 teabag (1 tblsp) chamomile tea
½ teaspoon cinnamon powder
½ teaspoon ginger powder
¾ cup boiling water
¾ cup honey

Place all the herbs into the water and let steep for half an hour.

Strain into a small saucepan and add honey. Clip thermometer to the side of the pan.

Bring to the boil and continue boiling until mixture reaches 300º. Watch carefully, it is really easy to burn when it gets this hot!

Remove from heat and allow to cool for 5-10 minutes, until it starts to get syrupy.

Drop by small spoonful's onto parchment paper and let cool. Dust with slippery elm bark, (or icing sugar) to prevent them from sticking together.

Store in an airtight container.

Honey in the Garden

If you are like me, you like to create plants from cuttings. I love to get some free plants, or to make sure that favourites are always in the garden.

Many years ago, someone told me that you could use honey to strike cuttings and I thought they were joking. But then I had a go and I was very surprised to find that it worked. And it worked just as well as any rooting powder that I had tried before.

It is a really easy process and where as you may run out of the rooting powder, you will usually have some honey in the cupboard.

When taking cuttings, I like to cut the stem just below a leaf, and leaving the top leaves in place, remove whatever is in the middle.

My cuttings, depending on the plant are usually around 5 cm in length.

Next, I'll put some honey on my finger, as shown in picture or else if I'm doing a few, I'll put about a tablespoon in a small container.

Dip the cutting into the honey, making sure that at least half a centre metre is covered.

Make a hole, using a stick, into the potting mix.

Then place the cutting carefully and push the soil around it.

Repeat until the pot is full of cuttings placed about 4 cms apart. Water. Leave in a place out of direct sun .

HONEY FERMENTATION

I love making flavoured honey. It can be used in so many ways. It adds some depth and creative flavourings to baked goods and drinks. It tastes delicious on toast as well. These are made in a similar way as an infused honey is made, however instead of using dried herbs, we use fresh.

Fill a clean jar up to the halfway point with your chosen fruit or vegetables that has been chopped up to small pieces. If you are making garlic honey, then hit the garlic cloves with the side of a knife.

Pour honey over the produce, (raw, organic, unfiltered is great) slowly.

Allow it time to sink down and thoroughly coat everything before you decide whether you need more.

(Note that it is totally normal at this stage for there to be floaters at the top. You don't need to keep adding honey.)

You want the jar to be around halfway to 2/3 full. As moisture is pulled from your produce, the water level will keep rising. A final honey-water level around 2/3 to 3/4 up the jar is ideal.

For the first week, it is recommended to either stir the ferment with a wooden spoon or turn the jar upside down every day, if not twice. (If turning upside down, seal it tightly and plan to keep it in a large bowl as honey can escape out the side.

Periodically, open the jar for the first week, as airborne yeasts are needed in this ferment.

For the next week or two, stirring or turning can be done less frequently, such as every second or third day.

After the first few weeks, you will notice the produce now sinks below the honey (and is noticeably darker) and the need to stir or turn the jar is essentially over.

You can leave it on the bench or in a cupboard as long as you like. Fermentation will be ongoing. It is safe to open the jar and taste it as you desire. If you achieve a flavour you love and want to halt fermentation place it in your fridge.

When the flavour is to your liking, you can remove some of the fruit, or vegetable and use it in your recipes.

These honeys can last for at least a year, but you will probably use them much quicker than that.

Fermented Garlic Honey

1 cup of peeled garlic cloves

3/4 cup raw honey

Hit the garlic cloves with the side of a knife or leave whole. (It's up to you)

Place in a clean jar.

Pour honey over the top.

See the main instructions for the method.

The Fermented Garlic Honey is very popular because it can be used in place of plain honey or garlic in a variety of recipes

Try adding it to a marinade for meats and vegetable

Use it when making sauces where you want a garlic and honey flavour.

Drizzle over a grilled steak instead of steak sauce.

Use it to make a vinaigrette for salads.

Chop up the garlic cloves and add to any dish or salads.

Fermented Honey Garlic Vinaigrette

1 cup Extra Virgin Olive Oil

1/3 cup Apple Cider Vinegar

3 tablespoons Fermented Garlic Honey

Mix all together. Let sit for about an hour before using to allow the flavours to blend.

Mix again before using.

Peach and Cinnamon Honey

Enough firm ripe peaches to half fill your jar.

1 Cinnamon Stick

Raw Honey

Peel and chop the firm peaches into smaller pieces. Place cinnamon stick on the bottom of your clean jar and cover with honey.

Follow instructions on previous page for process.

Apple and Ginger Fermented Honey

Enough Firm Ripe Apples to half fill your jar.

1 tablespoon grated Ginger

Raw Honey

Peel and chop the apples into small pieces and place in a clean jar with the grated ginger.

Cover with honey.

Follow instructions on previous page for process.

Berry Fermented Honey

Enough Firm Ripe Berries to half fill your jar.

Raw Honey

Cut berries or leave whole and place in a clean jar.

Cover with honey.

Follow instructions on previous page for process.

Beeswax

One of the most amazing by-products of harvesting the bee hives is all the beautiful beeswax. It's incredible just how much you have and finding ways to use it all is challenging.

However, Beeswax is a wonderful product, to have on hand around the house, because it can be used for a whole lot of handmade products.

Leather Polish

100 gms Macadamia nut Oil
25 gms beeswax

Melt in a pyrex jug set in water, over low heat.

Pour into tins. When cool place lids

(note: If making shoe polish try adding some pigment about 1.25gms)

Coating Nails & Screws
Once you coat your nails and screws with **beeswax**, they do not splinter the wood while you hammer them in.

Cheese Waxing
If you produce your own cheese, **beeswax** is the best natural cover for cheeses. If the cheese is wet, you will need to let it dry before applying the hot wax. This is to ensure a proper seal because wax will not adhere to wet surfaces. Beeswax works well for sealing the because it has a low melting point.

Waterproof Shoes and Boots
Rub the beeswax over the entire shoe. Next, use a blow dryer to melt the wax all over the shoe then let set for about 5 minutes before wearing.

Wood Lubricant
Rub beeswax on sliding glass doors, windows or drawers that tend to stick to restore smooth movement. Beeswax is also a fantastic lubricant for oiling very old furniture joints.

Prevent Rust
Coat things like hand tools, cast iron pieces and shovels to prevent them from rusting out. You can even rub **beeswax** on the wooden handle of your shovel to help protect against wear and tear.

Grease Biscuit Trays
If you have a block of wax, you can simply rub it over your pans and use it in place of butter or oil. (Beeswax is edible so this is perfectly safe.) It works best if you warm the sheet a bit first. You can also melt the wax and apply it that way. Over time the pan will take on a permanent coat of wax, eliminating the need to grease every time.

Beeswax Wraps

These are great to make to use in the kitchen and terrific gifts for the eco conscious friends and family. They are very easy. You will come across many ways to do them and so often expensive ingredients are called for, such as pine resin or jojoba oil. These aren't really necessary, I like to make these simple ones that only use beeswax and cloth.

I prefer to use cotton and buying cotton scrap material or clothes that can be cut up to make different sizes and shapes from op shops is a fantastic way to recycle. I have even used old sheets. Make sure they are very clean before you apply the wax.

Try to use colourful materials because you may as well make them pretty as well as useful.

The wraps are great to use instead of plastic film, like gladwrap. They mould over bowls and you can wrap cheese, bread or other food into them.

Over time, they may need re-waxing, but this is easily done. Have fun with these and show all your friends how to make them, I'm sure they will appreciate it, as they can be quite pricey to buy them.

WHAT YOU WILL NEED

100% pure beeswax
Clean 100% Cotton material
Pinking Shears
Parchment Paper
Biscuit Tray

HOW TO MAKE THE WRAPS

Cut material into different sizes and shapes to suit you.

Pre heat oven to low temp.

Place parchment paper onto tray.

Place material onto paper. If your material is one sided, place the patterned side facing down.

Evenly distribute beeswax pellets or shavings, (don't miss the edges)

Place tray into oven to melt the wax, which will take a couple of minutes, then spread the wax with the brush. Making sure it is evenly distributed.

Hang to dry and when it is no longer sticky it's ready.

Replace the paper each time you make a new one.

HOW TO CARE FOR YOUR WRAPS

Wash your wraps by hand in cool water with a mild dish soap. Place them on a drying rack or clothesline to dry. Avoid any heat such as hot water, microwaves, or ovens that will cause the beeswax to melt, ruining your wraps.

Beeswax Modelling Clay

Modelling clay is like plasticine. It's not too hard to make and it will last for ages. The kids will love playing with it.

You will need about 1/2 kilo of beeswax, about 5 tablespoons Olive Oil, about 4 teaspoons lanolin and some cheap soy crayons of different colours. The reason I say these measurements are 'about' is because depending on the beeswax and how hard it is, will depend on how much you will need of the other ingredients.

Melt the beeswax in a double boiler, add the oil and the lanolin. Allow to cool.

Take a scoop and play with it, it will gradually become supple as it warms in your hands. If its supple enough after a few minutes and doesn't crumble its ready for the next step. However if its not quite right, add another tablespoon of oil and a teaspoon of lanolin. If its too sticky, then just add the oil and not the lanolin. In the unlikely event that its TOO supple, then add more beeswax at a 1/4 cup at a time. When you're happy with how it is working you are ready to colour it.

Remelt the beeswax mix. Grate a crayon into a container that you won't want to use later. Add the beeswax mix and stir until the crayons are melted and evenly distributed. Pour into a paper lined muffin tin and allow them to cool. Repeat the process with different coloured crayons.

To use: Peel the paper away, and warm them in your hands until they are supple enough to shape. Sometimes this takes a few minutes, so warming them up in your own hands before giving them to the little kids is helpful for them.

Drawing Salve

This is great when you have a splinter. All you do is dab some on the spot, cover with a band-aid and leave overnight.

1/2 cup infused oil (comfrey, calendula, plantain are all good ones)

1 tablespoon beeswax pellets or shavings
2 tablespoons activated charcoal
2 tablespoons bentonite clay or kaolin clay
1/2 teaspoon vitamin E or use 1 capsule, optional, works as a preservative
20 drops lavender essential oil, optional, works as a skin soother
10 drops tea tree essential oil, optional, works as an antimicrobial and anti-inflammatory

In a pyrex jug, sitting in a saucepan, with water to half the jug, melt the beeswax in the oil.

Remove from heat and add all other ingredients, stirring until smooth.

Pour into tins and allow to cool before placing lid on.

Label and store in the cupboard.

Beeswax Sticks.

Melt beeswax and pour into ice cube trays that are shaped in a rectangle. I always the trays with vegetable oil before adding the wax.

Allow to cool before turning out.

Use them for:

Lubricating squeaky hinges

Lubricating zippers

Rubbing along wooden window edges to help them open and close

Rub along edges of garden tools to help keep them rust free.

DECIDE
WHAT KIND
OF LIFE
YOU REALLY
WANT...
AND THEN,
SAY NO
TO EVERYTHING
THAT ISN'T THAT

Nuts and Milks

Nut Milks

Nut milks have become popular over the last few years, especially with people who are lactose intolerant. But there are more reasons to use nut milks, instead of dairy milk. They offer health benefits. They are low in calories, which is a good thing if you are watching your weight. They provide a range of vitamins that our bodies need, that aren't present in dairy milk. They give a different taste to recipes you want to use them in. But the best thing in my eyes, is that if you have a preppers pantry, you can keep nuts and make the milk when you need to or if you can't get some dairy milk.

Instead of buying the pre processed nut milks from the supermarket, they are super easy to make at home. The other benefit of making them yourself, is that they won't have any of the additives, commercial ones have. They won't have any preservatives or thickeners added and they won't have the high price tag.

Nut milks taste great when added to coffee, smoothies, baked goods or on your muesli for breakfast. Once you've made the milk, dry out the pulp and make some flour. You don't need to waste anything.

Almond Milk

Almond milk seems to be the most popular nut milk that people know. It is super easy to make.

Take 1 cup of almonds and soak them overnight in some filtered clean water.

Drain the almonds

Peel the skins off by rubbing them with a cloth.

Add the almonds to a blender with 4 cups of filtered water and blitz until smooth and creamy.

Pour the mixture through a sieve and a muslin cloth.

Squeeze out the rest of the milk.

Refrigerate. This will keep for a few days.

Don't toss the Pulp

Once you have made the milk, turn the pulp into something useful.

Dry it in a dehydrator and then pulverise it in a food processor to get it finer.

Use it as a gluten free bread crumb or use it as a flour.

Instead of just limiting yourself to Almond Milk, try different nuts and even different seeds. The process is the same with all them. You may find that if the milk is too thick then add more water, if it is too thin add less water. Mix and match the ingredients and add in more to make your own signature milk.

Sunflower Milk

1 cup sunflower seeds, soaked over night in filtered water. (discard the soaking water)

Blend the soaked sunflower seeds with 4 cups of filtered water.

Strain all the milk out and refrigerate.

Rice Milk

1 cup cooked brown or white rice

Blend the rice with 4 cups filtered water.

Strain and refrigerate.

Dry the pulp to create rice flour.

Coconut Milk

1 cup desiccated coconut

Blend the rice with 4 cups filtered water.

Strain and refrigerate.

Dry the pulp to create coconut flour.

Coconut Cream

1 cup desiccated coconut

Blend the rice with 4 cups filtered water.

Strain and refrigerate.

The next day there will be separation.

Skim the cream from the top.

When you have finished making your nut milk you will have the pulp to deal with. Please don't throw it away. Turn it into butter or flour, or use it before dehydrating in recipes like cakes, biscuits or desserts.

Make flour from the pulp

Spread the pulp over a baking tray and place in a warm over (150c) for between 30 and 60 minutes.

Blend until flour like but be careful not to let it turn into butter.

Store in a glass container with an oxygen absorber.

It is best to store it in the fridge and use it sooner rather than later. Some nut flours go rancid quickly.

Make Nut Butter from the pulp.

Add the pulp to a blender and blend until it turns into butter.

If you feel the process requires a bit of oil, then try adding some macadamia oil, which won't too strong in its flavour.

This can sometimes take quite a bit of time, so you may have to rest your blender every few minutes.

Store in the fridge.

Roasted Nut Milk

If you are looking for a fuller flavour, try lightly roasting the nuts before you soak them.

Spread them out in a baking tray placed in a warm over for 15 minutes.

Stir them every 5 minutes.

Cool them on a tea towel or other cloth

Nut milk Ice Cream

This is something a bit different to make at home. Try different variations. My favourite is Chocolate Hazelnut using this recipe and adding 1 tablespoon of the best cacao powder you have.

2 cups nut milk of your choice
1/2 cup nut butter
1/3 cup sweetener (you can use sugar but try something different like date syrup, maple syrup, or rice syrup)
1/4 teaspoon fine sea or rock salt
1 1/2 teaspoons vanilla extract if making vanilla or chocolate ice cream. Or if you have other extracts use them to create something special.

Blend everything together and the then freeze using ice cube trays.

When frozen turn the cubes back into the blender and blend until smooth.

Refreeze if needed or serve immediately.

This recipe is best eaten the day it is made but you can refreeze it for up to a month and then thaw before eating.

Healthy Chocolate Milk

This tastes like Nutella, so you know the kids are going to love this as a treat.

1 cup hazelnuts (plus filtered water for overnight soak
4 cups filtered water
6-8 pitted dates
2 1/2 tablespoons cacao powder
1 1/2 teaspoons Vanilla extract
1/2 teaspoon fine sea or rock salt

Soak hazelnuts in filtered water over night. Discard water. Place nuts, water, dates, cacao powder, vanilla and salt into blender.
Blend until smooth.

Home made Nutella

Okay, the grandkids love Nutella, and one would assume it is healthy and good to eat, because it's sold in the supermarket, lol. But look at the ingredients and see what they put in it.

Now, I will share with you how to make a healthy version.

Firstly, make some Hazelnut milk by soaking 1 cup of hazelnuts in some water overnight then drain and rub the skins off, or leave them if you like. Place the nuts in a blender with 4 cups of water. Blend. Strain the milk and put the pulp back into the blender. Add 1 teaspoon Vanilla Extract, 1 teaspoon cacao, 1 tablespoon Maple Syrup, a good pinch sea salt, 1 teaspoon macadamia oil, and 1/4 cup Hazelnut milk. Blend until smooth.

Pistachio Nut Cheese

This isn't a real cheese but close enough. It will only keep for a few days so you need eat it.

1 cup shelled Pistachio Nuts (soaked overnight with a pinch of salt. Rinsed and drained)
1/2 cup Nutritional Yeast
1 tablespoon Maple Syrup
2 cloves Garlic
Juice from 1/2 lemon
1 tablespoon Apple Cider Vinegar
1 1/2 cups filtered water
1 tablespoon Agar Agar Powder
2 pinches fine sea or rock salt

To a blender add half the water and all the other ingredients except the Agar Agar.
Blend until smooth.

In a small saucepan add the rest of the water and the agar agar.
Simmer for 5 minutes, stirring constantly until the agar agar has no lumps.
Take off the stove and add the nut mixture and blend well.
Pour into a mould, lined with greaseproof paper and refrigerate for a few hours.

Unmould and serve with crackers.
Consume within 3 days.

Yummo Magnesium Rich Balls

24 fresh dates, pitted
½ cup (80g) almonds (or pulp from making milk)
1/4 cup pumpkin seeds
1 tablespoon raw honey (or maple syrup)
1 tablespoon coconut oil, melted
2 tablespoons raw cacao powder
1/2 teaspoon sea salt flakes

Blend all the ingredients except the white powder and coconut.

Roll into balls and coat with coconut.

Refrigerate for a couple of hours and enjoy.

Note: you can add anything you like to this basic blend. I often add Chia seeds, sunflower seeds, my white powder or cinnamon.

This snack is full of magnesium rich food and you wouldn't realise you were eating something that is super good for you. Another great way to get fussy eaters to eat well.

Going back to a simpler life is not a step backward

Yvon Chouinard

Make these from scratch too

Sweetened Condensed Milk

1/2 cup Boiling Water
1 tablespoon Butter
1 cup Sugar
1 cup powdered milk

Put the milk and sugar into a blender.

Melt the butter into the boiling water.

Pour the butter/water into the blender and blend until the sugar has dissolved. You will probably need to scrape the sides down occasionally.

It will thicken as it cools. Store in the fridge for a week to 10 days.

Golden Syrup

In a heavy based saucepan heat 1/2 cup sugar and 1/4 cup water over medium to low heat until the sugar has dissolved.

Bring to a simmer until it has caramelised. Brush down any sugar from the sides so that it doesn't crystallise .

Add 2 1/4 cups sugar and 1 tablespoon lemon juice. Whisk and slowly and carefully add 1 1/2 cups boiling water (it has to be boiling) until the sugar dissolves.

Allow to simmer for 17-20 minutes over medium/low heat.

Mayonnaise (this is a very easy one)

1 egg
200 grams Extra Virgin Olive Oil
1 tablespoon lemon juice
1/4 teaspoon salt
1 teaspoon Dijon mustard

Blend all until emulsified.

Keep in the fridge

Lemon Pepper Seasoning

6 tablespoons dried, powdered, lemon peel

2 tablespoons coarse ground black pepper

2 teaspoons sea salt

2 teaspoons onion powder

1¼ teaspoon garlic powder

Mix all and keep in a jar.

Garlic Aioli

2 teaspoons lemon juice

1 egg yolk, at room temperature

1 clove garlic, minced and mashed into a paste

1 cup extra-virgin olive oil

sea salt, to taste

Beat lemon juice, egg yolk, and garlic until well combined.

While whisking vigorously, drizzle a few drops of oil into bowl with egg mixture. Still whisking, drizzle in a few more drops, and continue to whisk vigorously until egg mixture is very thick and emulsified. Gradually add remaining oil in a very thin stream while whisking vigorously until the aïoli is smooth, pale yellow, and emulsified. Season with salt.

Keep, refrigerated and covered, for up to 3 days.

Tartare Sauce

½ cup mayonnaise	1 teaspoon mustard
¼ teaspoon onion powder	¼ teaspoon garlic powder
2 tablespoons small diced gherkins	
1 tablespoon capers	1 tablespoon lemon juice
1 pinch salt and pepper	1 pinch freshly ground black pepper,

Use a blender to create a smooth sauce.

Keeps for about a week in the refrigerator.

Worcestershire Sauce

1 cup apple cider vinegar

¼ cup molasses

¼ cup soy sauce

3 tablespoons honey

1½ tablespoons fish sauce

2 teaspoons freshly ground black pepper

2 cloves garlic

2 teaspoons onion powder

1 teaspoon chilli powder

½ teaspoon ground cinnamon, or ground cloves

1 teaspoon ground ginger

juice of 1 lime

In a small saucepan, mix ingredients together and bring to a boil.

Reduce heat and simmer for 10 minutes.

Remove from heat and pour into a blender.

Blend until smooth.

Store in a bottle or covered bowl in the refrigerator for up to 1 month.

Tzatziki

2 cups grated cucumber

1 teaspoon salt

1 cup greek yogurt

1 large garlic clove, finely minced

3 tablespoons chopped fresh dill or mint (or a combo of both)

1/4 –1/2 teaspoon salt and pepper to taste

a squeeze of lemon to taste

Place cucumber and the 1 teaspoon of salt in a bowl and let sit for 10 minutes. Rinse well under cold water. Press all the juice out and you will have about a cup of cucumber left.

Blend all ingredients except the cucumber.

Fold the cucumber through the mix.

Keep refrigerated. Will last about 4 days.

Super White Powder

Okay it's not really blisteringly white, but a kind of beige colour, but it is full or the most amazing super foods. Everybody needs to figure out ways to get more nutrients into their diets and if you are like me there is just so much I can fit into my meals every day. I like to come up with ideas that help me get the most vitamins and minerals into us without us even realising that we are doing it. This is also a terrific idea for finnicky eaters or kids or elderly people.

This powder has the following ingredients:

Linseeds (flax seeds), Sunflower seeds, Almonds, Pumpkin seeds and Quinoa flakes.

To make it just add equal amounts and blend it up until it's in powder form. Store it in a glass jar, in the fridge. Or use the dehydrated pulp from your nut and seed milks.

Now, why have I added these particular ingredients? Well the first three, you have recognised as the traditional LSA mix and I added the others because they are super awesome as well, so why not pack as much into the powder as we can.

Linseeds, Sunflower seeds and Almonds (LSA), is an easy, extremely versatile way to add extra nutrients to meals. LSA is rich in protein, which helps to keep your blood-sugar levels balanced and curb sugar cravings. LSA will provide you with a rich source of omega-3, omega-6 and omega-9. This will help to promote a healthy heart and brain function, and it contains important minerals such as calcium, zinc and magnesium.

Pumpkin seeds have a wide variety of nutrients ranging from magnesium and manganese to copper, protein and zinc, pumpkin seeds are nutritional powerhouses wrapped up in a very small package. They also contain plant compounds known as phytosterols and free-radical scavenging antioxidants,1 which can give your health an added boost. Because these are high-fibre seeds, they're able to boost your fiber intake

Quinoa contains more protein than any other grain. It can help lower cholesterol levels as it is a great source of fibre and helps to promote cardiovascular health. Quinoa contains a range of important nutrients, such as iron and B vitamins, for red blood cell production and energy; calcium, for strong bones; magnesium, for nervous system health; and vitamin E, a powerful antioxidant. It's also an ideal grain for diabetics as it has a low glycaemic index, which will help keep blood-sugar levels stable and prevent sharp spikes in insulin. You can use quinoa as a substitute for rice.

So, as you can see this powder is chockers full of the good stuff and so easy to include in your daily food.

I like to add a tablespoon to my smoothies, but you can add some to just about every dish you make. Try adding a tablespoon or two to sweet or savoury dishes. The flavour is not overpowering, so the powder can be added to just about anything you can think of. Try some in your next home made pizza dough, biscuits, cakes, stews, desserts, sauces or just about anything. You can even sprinkle it on your yogurt and fruit, or muesli.

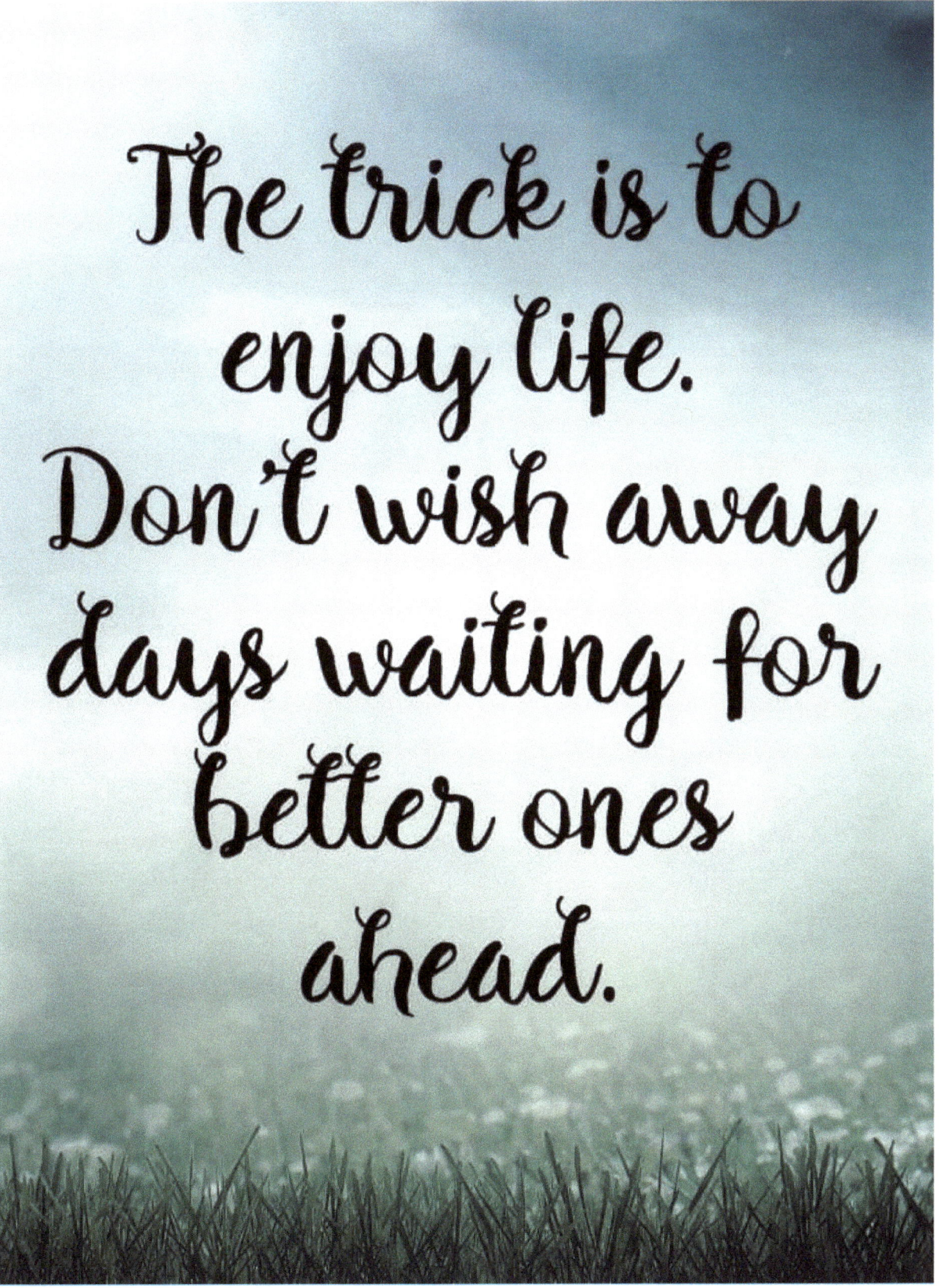

Natural Household Cleaning

Natural Household Cleaning

Today's modern home is loaded with toxic and polluting substances designed to make domestic life easier. But, the cost of these commercial, chemical-based products can be high. These products have long term health concerns for the family, and environmental pollution caused by their manufacture and disposal. In Australia, for example, many, many people suffer from allergies, asthma, sinusitis or bronchitis. Treatment for these conditions should include reducing synthetic chemicals in the home environment.

For many home-cleaning chores, you can make your own cleaning products using some of the recipes that follow.

A growing number of commercial non-toxic home cleaning products are also available, as healthier and environmentally responsible alternatives. Your use of these products helps promote the growth of green businesses which are contributing to a sustainable economy. When I want to buy any products, I will only do so from companies that I trust. I am a Wellness Advocate with Doterra. Here is my website: mydoterra.com/offthegridinoz.

Homemade Substitutions

There are many inexpensive, easy-to-use natural alternatives which can safely be used in place of commercial household products. Here is a list of common, environmentally safe products which can be used alone or in combination for a wealth of household applications.

Bi Carb- cleans, deodorizes, softens water, scours.

Soap - unscented soap in liquid form, flakes, powders or bars is biodegradable and will clean just about anything. Avoid using soaps which contain petroleum distillates.

Lemon - one of the strongest food-acids, effective against most household bacteria.

White Vinegar - cuts grease, removes mildew, odours, some stains and wax build-up.

Washing Soda - or SAL Soda is sodium carbonate decahydrate, a mineral. Washing soda cuts grease, removes stains, softens water, cleans walls, tiles, sinks and tubs. Use care, as washing soda can irritate mucous membranes. Do not use on aluminium.

Corn Flour - can be used to clean windows, polish furniture, shampoo carpets and rugs.

Essential Oils - These are wonderful and can be used in so many ways around the house. There isn't too many things I do at home, whether it be for cleaning the house, keeping bugs and vermin at bay, or keeping us healthy, where I don't include essential oils. Please see below to buy Doterra essential oils at wholesale prices to save you 25% off retail price. I only use and recommend Doterra for a lot of reasons. I trust Doterra Essential Oils.

Borax - (sodium borate) cleans, deodorizes, disinfects, softens water, cleans wallpaper, painted walls and floors. One question that gets asked a lot ... Is Borax Safe? Borax is considered a mild skin irritant similar to baking soda. The MSDS lists borax as a health hazard of 1, similar to salt and baking soda. A health concern with borax is with its potential to disrupt the reproductive system. Studies have not been done in humans regarding this; however, potential reproductive issues in mice are suspected from high levels of ingested borax. Use of borax for home cleaning formulas, where no borax is ingested, has not been shown to pose health hazards. Borax is a natural substance which is non-carcinogenic, does not accumulate in the body, or absorb through the skin. It is not harmful to the environment.

> A lot of how I clean these days includes essential oils. I find them not just worthwhile because they work well, but just the shear fact that they smell delicious, which can help make the sometimes thankless task of keeping the home healthy and clean, by giving us some joy at the same time. I am a Doterra Wellness Advocate and love their products. If you would like to purchase them for yourself visit https://www.mydoterra.com/offthegridinoz I find that becoming a wholesale customer is a great option to save money.

Natural Household Cleaners

Laundry Detergent

Mix 1 cup Earth Dishwashing liquid, 1/2 cup washing soda and 1/2 cup borax.
Use 1 tbsp for light loads; 2 tbsp for heavy loads

Washing powder

2 kilo bi carbonate soda
100 ml eucalyptus oil
200 ml water

Stir to combine.....
Store in a dry container.
Use a couple of tablespoons per wash.

(thanks to Sally Baker)

Washing Powder

1 Bar Laundry soap grated
1 cup Borax
1 cup Washing Soda
35 drops Lavender or Eucalyptus Essential Oil

Mix all together well
Store in a dry container
Use 1 to 3 tablespoons per wash.

To make the mix more powdery you can use a blender, but make sure you grate the soap first.

Natural Cockroach Help

Ahhh the dreaded cockroach. They aren't very pretty and we don't like to watch them scurrying around the kitchen. Keeping food in containers and out of their reach is good plus we keep our plates, bowls, saucepans etc upside down so they can't crawl around them.

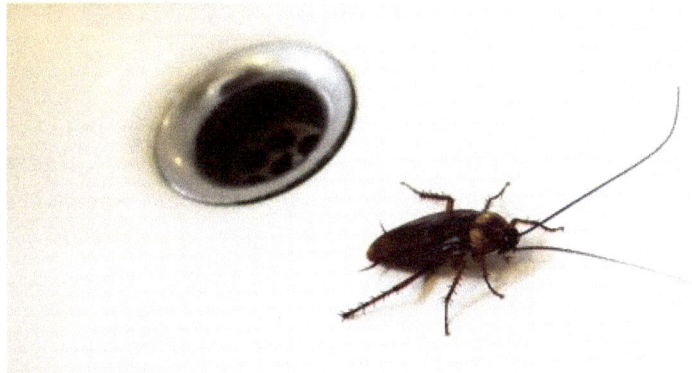

If you have a problem with cockroaches, one very easy remedy is to use some Bi Carbonate Soda mixed with some icing sugar, in some little containers that the roaches can get to. Works well with nothing to worry other critters.

Another natural idea is to add a couple of drops of essential oils to a spray bottle with some water. Salt added to this can help as well. Just spray it around places that you know they like to be, such as under the refrigerator.

Essential oils, like Peppermint, Tea Tree, Cypress or Eucalyptus work well.

ALL PURPOSE CLEANER

¼ cup white vinegar, 1 tablespoon liquid soap, 1 ¾ cups water, 30 drops essential oils. I like 15 drops each of Lavender and Lemon but I sometimes change it to 10 drops each of Eucalyptus, Peppermint, and Wild Orange or 30 drops Doterra On Guard®, or 15 drops each of Grapefruit and Doterra On Guard. Add all ingredients to 500ml spray bottle. Shake thoroughly.

DISINFECTANT

¼ cup white vinegar. 1 ¾ cups water. 30 drops Doterra essential oils. I recommend these essential oil combinations: 15 drops each of Lavender and Lemon, 10 drops each of Eucalyptus, Peppermint, and Wild Orange, 30 drops Doterra On Guard, 15 drops each of Grapefruit and Doterra On Guard. Instructions Add all ingredients to 500ml spray bottle. Shake thoroughly.

AIR FRESHENER

Commercial air fresheners mask smells and coat nasal passages to diminish the sense of smell. Bi Carb or vinegar with lemon juice in small dishes absorbs odours around the house. Having houseplants helps reduce odours in the home. Prevent cooking odours by simmering vinegar (1 tbsp in 1 cup water) on the stove while cooking. To get such smells as fish and onion off utensils and cutting boards, wipe them with vinegar and wash in soapy water. Keep fresh coffee grounds on the counter. Simmer water and cinnamon or other spices on stove. Place bowls of fragrant dried herbs and flowers in room.

My favourite ways: Diffuse 5 drops of Doterra's Purify Essential Oil blend with 5 drops of Lemon Essential Oil as air fresheners. Make a spray air freshener by adding 20 drops each Doterra's Purify blend and Lemon Essential oil to a 500ml spray bottle, add 1 tablespoon or vodka and top with water.

FURNITURE POLISH

¼ cup olive oil, ¼ cup vinegar, 10 drops doTERRA essential oils I love Wild Orange, Arborvitae, or Lemon. Add olive oil and vinegar to glass spray bottle. Add 10 drops of essential oil. Shake well before each use. Apply to microfiber cloth and wipe wood surfaces clean. Repeat every two to three months or as often as needed.

OVEN CLEANER

Bicarb, Water, 6 drops Doterra Lemon essential oil, 6 drops Doterra Lime essential oil. Mix a paste of bicarb, water and Lemon & Lime essential oils. Coat the oven surfaces with the paste (avoiding bare metal and heating elements), let stand overnight. Use a plastic spatula to remove the paste. Wipe away any remaining residue with a clean, wet sponge.

NON SCRATCH SCOURING POWDER

¼ cup bicarb, ¼ cup table salt, 1 tablespoon vinegar, 2 tablespoons water, 4–5 drops of Doterra's Purify Cleansing Blend. Stir all ingredients together until they form a paste and spread it over the stove top and burners. Leave it on for 15 minutes or longer for hard-to-remove stains. Using a sponge, scrub the mixture into the grime. Remove excess cleaner and wipe surface clean.

WINDOW CLEANER

Mix 2 teaspoons of white vinegar with 1 litre warm water. Use crumpled newspaper or cotton cloth to clean. Only use the black and white newspapers, not the coloured ones. Don't clean windows if the sun is on them, or if they are warm, or streaks will show on drying. Be sure to follow the recipe, because using too strong a solution of vinegar will etch the glass and eventually cloud it. Add a few drops of lemon, peppermint or other essential oil of your choice.

CITRUS VINEGAR

Make your own citrus vinegar to use in place of the normal white vinegar. This is easy and gives your cleaning jobs an extra bit of oomph. Place citrus skins into white vinegar and let sit for a few weeks. Use in place of regular vinegar.

DISHWASHER TABLETS

1 cup bi carb, ¼ cup citric acid, 1 tablespoon Doterra On Guard Cleaner Concentrate, 5 drops Grapefruit essential oil. Put bi carb, citric acid, Doterra On Guard Cleaner Concentrate, and Grapefruit oil in a mixing bowl. Mix together until the mixture is an even consistency. Place in silicon moulds and let sit for four hours. Remove tablets. Store in an airtight container. Use in dishwasher in place of store-bought dishwasher tablets.

SHOE DEODORISER

The everyday shoes we wear to exercise, play, and run errands in are bound to start smelling at some point. Rather than banish them outside or having to wash them in your washer, put essential oils to the task to give your shoes a refresh. ½ cup rubbing alcohol, 20 drops Tea Tree (Melaleuca) oil, 20 drops Cypress oil, 20 drops Lemon oil. In a small spray bottle, add rubbing alcohol, Tea Tree, Cypress, and Lemon oils. Close the bottle and shake well to combine. Remove the shoe soles then spray the inside of smelly shoes. Let dry. Enjoy the smell of clean shoes. Another tried and true method is to place 1 dessertspoon of bicarbonate soda mixed with a few drops of essential oils. Leave overnight and shake to empty.

TOILET BOWL CLEANER (3 recipes)

1) Mix 1/4 cup bicarb and 1 cup vinegar, pour into basin and let it set for a few minutes. Scrub with brush and rinse.

2) A mixture of borax (2 parts) and lemon juice (one part).

3) 1/2 cup bicarb, 1/3 cup liquid dishwashing soap, 1/4 cup hydrogen peroxide, 30 drops eucalyptus essential oil, 3/4 cup water. Mix together in a squeeze-type bottle, then squirt into toilet. Scrub and let stand 20 minutes. Rinse off.

WOOD FURNITURE POLISH

Bring back the shine to your favourite tables, countertops, floors, and more with this simple recipe for homemade wood polish with essential oils. ¼ cup olive oil, ¼ cup vinegar, 10 drops Doterra essential oils (Wild Orange, Arborvitae, or Lemon). Add olive oil and vinegar to glass spray bottle. Add 10 drops of essential oil. Shake well before each use. Apply to microfiber cloth and wipe wood surfaces clean. Repeat every 2–3 months or as often as needed.

TUB AND TILE CLEANERS

Cleaning the bathroom is not an experience people look forward to very often. Being stuck in a small closed space with harsh chemicals not only makes it hard to breathe but can also be hazardous to your health. The next time you clean your bathroom, why not try mixing up an effective cleaner with many ingredients you already have at home. It still might not be your favourite household chore, but you will at least have a clean bathroom cleaning product to make the job a little easier to handle.

For simple cleaning, rub in bicarb with a damp sponge and rinse with fresh water.

For tougher jobs, wipe surfaces with vinegar first and follow with bicarb as a scouring powder. (Vinegar can break down tile grout, so use sparingly.

Soft Scrub for Bath, Tile, or Toilet,

Make in small batches and store in an airtight container. This is enough for two to four applications. This soft scrub is excellent for getting rid of soap scum, removing stains, and brightening your tiles and toilet. To use, just apply and let it sit for 5–10 minutes and then scrub. Once done scrubbing, take a wet cloth and wipe clean.

¾ cup bicarb, ¼ cup unscented liquid castile soap or Earth Dishwashing Liquid, 1 tablespoon water, 1 tablespoon vinegar, 5–10 drops Lemon essential oil.

Note: This scrub is also great to use to help clean your kitchen sink, refrigerator, or tile floors.

FLOOR CLEANERS

Disinfecting Floor Cleaner

To every bucket of warm water add 1/2 cup white vinegar, 1/2 cup borax, 1 teaspoon liquid castile soap, 10 drops each Lemon and Peppermint Essential Oils

General Floor Cleaner

To every bucket of warm water add 1/2 cup white vinegar, 1 teaspoon Liquid Castile Soap and 10 drops each Lemon and Peppermint Essential Oil.

Laminate Floor Cleaner

To every bucket of warm water add 1/2 cup white vinegar and 10 drops each Lemon and Peppermint essential oils.

Wood Floor Cleaner

To every bucket of warm water add 1/2 cup olive oil, 1/2 cup vinegar and 20 drops Lemon Essential Oil or 1/2 cup Lemon Juice. Keep one mop for these floors.

CORNFLOUR CLEANING!

Did you know that cornflour can be used for cleaning? In Australia Cornflour is usually derived from wheat but we still call it Cornflour and in the US cornflour is called Cornstarch. So now we are all totally confused but if you want to try something different that you will already have in your cupboard then give some of these ideas a try. Cornflour is good for more than just cleaning.

Apply cornflour to grease stains on fabric and leave for 12 hours. Remove and wash as normal.

A paste of cornflour and water can be used to clean silver.

Sprinkle cornflour on your carpet and wait 30 minutes then vacuum.

Use a little cornflour on a buffing rag to shine your car.

Sprinkle cornflour on grease stains on leather and let sit overnight. Brush away.

Mix two teaspoon cornflour with two teaspoons liquid soap. Add to bucket of warm water. Use this mixture to clean your windows.

A thick paste of cornflour and water can be applied to crayon marks on your walls. Apply paste and allow to dry completely. Then just wipe away.

Mix cornflour 3 to 1 with water to form a paste. Use as a substitute for a soft scrub type product. This can be used to clean stove tops, hoods, etc.

Remove grease spots from wallpaper by applying a thick paste of cornflour and water. Allow to dry then brush away.

After polishing your wood furniture, add a small amount of cornflour and buff. This will make a great shine.

Remove soap scum with a mixture of 1 cup vinegar, 1 tablespoon cornflour, and 2 tablespoons liquid soap.

Mix 2 teaspoons cornflour with 1/4 cup bicarb soda and a few drops of essential oil for scent. Add a teaspoon to the dryer for a alternative fabric softener.

For mould and mildew stains, mix 1 teaspoon cornflour, 1 tablespoon bicarb soda, 1 teaspoon lemon juice, and 1/4 cup of water.

Scrub your pots and pans with a bit of cornflour to bring back the shine.

Apply a bit of cornflour to knots to loosen.

Clean urine stains by applying a thick paste of corn starch and water. Allow to dry completely then brush or vacuum away.

Stains on fabrics (blood, ink, scorch marks, etc) can often be removed by applying a thick paste of cornflour and water to the area. Allow to dry then remove.

Sprinkle cornflour in between squeaky floor boards to eliminate the noise.

Sprinkle cornflour in shoes to absorb perspiration and odours.

Household Fire Lighters

Although not cleaning products, if you rely on a fire to keep you warm in the winter, or use a combustion stove for your cooking, you will no doubt want ways to light the fire without having to use those smelly commercial firelighters. We seem to have acquired a box of cheap candles from somewhere in our travels. Now while these can be useful if the lights go out, the fact that the lights don't go out that often a whole box of candles are just sitting there, so I decided to put them to a practical use. If you have a lot of beeswax, you can also use that.

There are a few ways to make some firelighters for yourself, using different things around the property so you won't have to spend money to create them. And you can get creative too and give some as gifts to friends.

Candle Wax and dried twigs

Gather some dry twigs.

Melt the candles in a glass pyrex jug sitting in some water on the stove.

Pour some of the wax over the twigs and allow to dry.

Candle Wax and drier lint

Put that lint collected in the drier to good use. Melt the candles in a glass pyrex jug sitting in some water on the stove.

Place the lint into an empty egg container. Pour over wax to just cover the lint.

When dry, cut each piece to use.

Candle Wax and corks

Put those old corks to a worthwhile cause.

Melt the candles in a glass pyrex jug sitting in some water on the stove.

Pour some of the wax over each cork and allow to dry.

Toilet Paper Tubes and newspaper

Scrunch up newspaper and fill the tube, leaving a paper wick coming from one side.

Cake papers and wood shavings

Fill cake papers with wood shavings.

Pour over hot wax and allow to dry.

Egg Containers

Half fill egg containers with dried pine needles, wood shavings, or drier lint.

Melt a candle or beeswax in a glass pyrex jug sitting in some water on the stove.

Pour over and allow to dry.

Citrus Peels

Dried citrus peels work well on their own, however, filling a half a dried lemon or orange peel with some wood shavings, very small twigs, drier lint or pine needles and then covering them with hot wax and allowing them to dry out, works even better.

Cotton Wool Balls and Vaseline

Dip a cotton wool ball into some Vaseline and place with the kindling to start the fire.

Herbs and Natural Products

Herbal Infused Oils

One of my favourite creative projects is to infuse oils. There are so many amazing things you can create with the end product because they are not just good for cooking or for using as a dressing on salad, but they can also be used as skin healers or hair treatments. And let's face it, having a range of these bottles lined up in the kitchen looks amazing and give such a lovely rustic look. They make great gifts too and not too expensive.

They are very easy to make and I always like to do the traditional method, where the herbs infuse in the oil for weeks. Some people like to use heat to quicken the process, and yes this can be good if you are in a hurry, but in my opinion it isn't as good. Patience is the key.

Using different oils to infuse the herbs into will also create different tastes or different uses, depending on what you are looking for.

The most common oil used is Extra Virgin Olive Oil which is readily available, however, I also like to use Avacado Oil, Grapeseed Oil, Sweet Almond Oil and Sunflower Oil. I never use Canola or Vegetable Oil however.

You can use many different herbs, fruits and spices to create your own signature oil. The most important thing to remember is when you are creating your herbal oils, using the slow traditional method, **NEVER** use fresh herbs because they have water in them and the oil will go rancid quickly. If you only have fresh herbs and need to make your oil for immediate use, then try the super quick method and use within a day or two.

Note:

I suggest that you always do your own research on which herbs to use if you are wanting to create a remedy.

I have been using different herbs for many years and always research first.

Some herbs are not to be used when pregnant others may be counter productive if you are taking medications.

If you are concerned , ask your doctor or

Traditional Method for creating Herbal Oils

Ingredients:

Extra Virgin Olive Oil
Dried herbs of your choice.

Method:

Fill jar with herbs and cover with oil.

Let sit for at least 2 weeks, but I prefer to let them sit for 6 to 8 weeks. I f you have space on a window sill, this is perfect.

Strain, bottle and label.

Slow Cooker Method for creating Herbal Oils

Ingredients:

Extra Virgin Olive Oil
Dried herbs of your choice.

Method:

Fill jar with herbs and cover with oil.

Place uncovered jar on to a tea towel that is sitting in warm water up to 3/4 the height of the jar, in a slow cooker on low heat. Let sit for 10-12 hours. Strain, bottle and label.

Oven Method for creating Herbal Oils

Ingredients:

Extra Virgin Olive Oil
Dried herbs of your choice.

Method:

In a pan cover herbs with oil.

Place in an oven warmed to 160C.

Turn oven off and let sit for 3 or 4 hours.

Strain, bottle and label

Super Quick Herbal Oils

Ingredients:
Extra Virgin Olive Oil
Herbs of choice

Method:
Blend all ingredients in a blender until smooth.
Strain and use immediately.
You can refrigerate this oil, but it needs to be used within a week.

(This is a good method to use when you only have fresh ingredients and want to create something delicious to have on a salad. I would never use this method to create a herbal oil that I wanted to keep or to use in balms.   )

Some Favourite Infused Oils are:

Chilli
Garlic
Rosemary
Lemon

Be adventurous, try...

Coriander
Onion
Mustard
Pepper
Cumin

Or even better add a couple.

Comfrey Oil

Follow the instructions for Calendula Oil, but use dried organic Comfrey Leaves.

I like to use the Comfrey oil in skin healing balms and creams and also in my pain balm.

Rosemary Oil

Follow the instructions for Calendula Oil, but use dried organic Rosemary.

I like to use this oil as a warm oil hair treatment.

Just apply about a tablespoon of Rosemary Oil to your hair and massage in. Leave it for at least half an hour then wash hair as normal.

Calendula Oil

Fill a jar with Dried Calendula Flowers. Cover with oil of choice, such as Extra Virgin Olive Oil.

Place in a dark place for about 8 weeks.

Strain into a clean amber bottle. Label and store in a dark place.

I like to use the Calendula oil in skin healing balms and creams..

It is a must have in any baby products like nappy rash cream.

Make your own Hydrosol (Flower Water)

Making essential oils can be done at home, but from my experiences of trying it, I have never had enough plant material, or the actual still to make it worthwhile. What I have done instead is make my own hydrosols. Hydrosols are the water that is created from the steaming process, that has captured the essential oil. The essential oils are infused into the water, giving you a beautiful, delicious, aromatic water.

The hydrosols can you used in so many ways and last a long, long time usually. They are easy to make and you can create quite a lot with less plant material. You can easily make citrus hydrosols using lemon or orange peels or rose or lavender or basil, okay you get the picture, you can make hydrosols from any plant that creates its own oil. Please remember, don't use any poisonous plants, and if you are unsure, then research it first.

I like to use the hydrosols in place of plain water in some recipes, such as orange hydrosol in jelly or lavender hydrosol in an icing for a special cake. The hydrosols are great as a spritz or can be added to other products to create things like a mosquito repellent. Let your imagination go wild and have some fun with this.

How to make your own Hydrosol

You will need a saucepan that can incorporate a steamer, a pyrex jug, water, fresh plant material and ice. If you don't have a steamer, you can use a flat rock or brick.

Fill bottom of saucepan with water and place steamer inside or use the rock and fill to cover it.

Place jug into the centre and place all the plant material that you are using around the jug.

Place the lid, upside down onto the saucepan.

Place ice on top of lid. Bring to boil and then allow to simmer. Keep adding ice as it melts.

The ice creates the evaporation of the steam that is capturing the oils and they will drip into the jug.

Be careful when removing the jug, because it will be hot.

When the hydrosol is cool, store in a dark glass bottle a store in a cupboard.

I love hydrosols made from roses, lavender, basil, aniseed, geranium, orange and lemons, eucalyptus, mint, lemon verbena, rosemary, sage, fennel, jasmine, chamomile, lemon grass, lemon balm, oh the list is endless.

Face Mist:

For a great little pick-me-up, spritz your face. It's refreshing and nourishing at any time. Rosemary hydrosol is great for enhancing your memory and keeping your mental focus sharp, lemon verbena is a great mood enhancer and very calming. Each plant will have different properties. Hydrosols will counteract drying and nourish your skin

Air Freshener:

Spritz your room to freshen and purify the air in your home. Add hydrosol to spray botte and spritz away.

Mosquito Repellent

15 drops lemongrass essential oil
10 drops eucalyptus essential oil
5 drops peppermint essential oil
4 drops tea tree essential oil
2 drops rosemary essential oil
2 drops cinnamon essential oil
1 drops lavender essential oil
1 1/4 tsp fractionated coconut oil

Hydrosol of choice:

In a 100ml glass spray bottle, add all oils and then fill to the top with hydrosol. Shake well before each use.

Rose Jelly

1 cup boiling water
250 gr sugar
3 to 4 Tablespoons rose water
a few drops red food colouring
3 teaspoons powdered gelatine

Dissolve sugar and gelatine in water.
Add rose water and food colouring.

Let set in refrigerator

Diffusing:

Add the hydrosol of choice to an ultrasonic (cold air) diffuser. This is a great way to get a gentle, aromatic and peaceful feeling to your home.

I like to add eucalyptus hydrosol to the diffuser when we are fighting off colds along with a couple of drops of Doterra's OnGuard essential oil

Stay cool:

Stay cool by spritzing peppermint hydrosol onto your face and body.

Keep Calm:

Spritz with chamomile, lavender or lemon balm hydrosol

Linen Spray:

Use the hydrosol of your choice to lightly spray the bed before sleeping.

Dog Bed Spray:

Lightly spray the dog bed with lavender hydrosol.

Focus Spray:

Spritz your face with rosemary hydrosol when you need to concentrate.

Exotic Marshmallows

Olive oil spray
½ cup icing sugar, plus more for dusting
15 gms powdered gelatine
2 large egg whites
2 cups sugar
¼ teaspoon hydrosol
1 drop food colouring (optional)

Combine gelatine and ½ cup cold water in a small bowl. Let stand until gelatine has softened, 10–15 minutes.

Using an electric mixer on medium-high speed, beat egg whites until soft peaks form, about 3 minutes.

Meanwhile, fit a medium heavy saucepan with thermometer. Bring sugar and ½ cup water to a boil over medium-high heat, stirring to dissolve sugar and brushing down sides with a wet pastry brush. Boil sugar mixture, without stirring, until thermometer registers 250°, 8–10 minutes. Remove from heat and add gelatine mixture, stirring until dissolved.

With mixer running, drizzle hot sugar mixture down side of bowl into egg whites; add rose water, increase speed to high, and beat until mixture has cooled slightly and tripled in volume, 5–7 minutes. Beat in food colouring, if desired. Spread marshmallow mixture into pan that has been sprayed with olive oils spray and dusted with icing sugar. Let cool at least 4 hours or overnight.

Dust tops of marshmallow with remaining ¼ cup powdered sugar. Turn out of pan and cut into 1" pieces; dust with more powdered sugar.

Interesting Fact:

You may come across the word Hydrosol, Hydrolat, Hydrolate, or Floral Waters when you are looking at recipes on the internet. They are more or less interchangeable these days for what I call Hydrosols.

Please note:

Adding essential oils to water does not create a hydrosol. The water created from the distilling, is a pure version an a lot safer to use.

Get experimenting.

If you keep in mind that a little goes a long way, AND you are only going to use plants and herbs that are not poisonous AND you know which ones are good to eat, then you can have so much fun creating new recipes that you can hand down to your grandchildren.

Try adding 1 teaspoon of your favourite hydrosol to a biscuit mix.

Or try adding 1/2 teaspoon when whipping cream to give yourself a treat with your apple pie. I like lemon hydrosol for this.

Try adding some lavender hydrosol to your bath when you need some special me time.

Salad Dressing.

1/4 cup olive oil
3 tablespoons fresh lemon juice
2 cloves garlic, crushed
2 teaspoons orange hydrosol, or get adventurous and try another one of your favourites
1 teaspoon honey or maple syrup
1/4 teaspoon ground cinnamon (optional)
salt and freshly ground pepper

Blend all together and use on your favourite salad.

Hair Rinse

4 teaspoons Apple Cider Vinegar
2 tablespoon Rosemary Hydrosol
2 tablespoon Lavender Hydrosol
Add above to a 100ml plastic bottle,
Fill with clean water. Shake to mix.

After shampooing use above, leave in for 2 minutes then rinse out with warm water.

Face mask

Many people love making their own face masks using different clays.

Try turning the clay into the mask using your hydrosols instead of plain water.

These work a treat. Use your favourite clays and add small amounts of the hydrosol until you have achieved the right texture for you.

Geranium Moisturiser

Geranium is great for you skin.

A really quick way to create a special moisturiser is to add 1/2 teaspoon of geranium hydrosol to about 50 grams of a natural moisture and blend well.

Keep this in the fridge.

Room Spray

100ml Sage Hydrosol or any others that you like
12 drops peppermint essential oil
8 drops lemon essential oil
4 drops lavender essential oil

Place all ingredients in a glass spray bottle and shake.

Herbal Infused Vinegars

Everybody loves to dress up their salads, well at least I do. Making a healthy, herbal vinegar is very easy to do and you will get the benefits from not just the Apple Cider Vinegar, but also the herbs that you add to it. These vinegars make lovely gifts, especially for the foodie in the family.

Herbal vinegars are not just for the kitchen though. Try making a lemon herbal infused vinegar for cleaning or a Herbal Hair Rinse.

I use Apple Cider Vinegar for most recipes, except for the household cleaning ones where I will use White Vinegar. If you do prefer the Red Wine Vinegar for some herbs that can be substituted too.

How to make an Infused Vinegar.

Place herbs into a jar and cover with vinegar.

Let sit for at least 2 weeks.

Strain, bottle and label.

That's it!!!

To use these herbal vinegars you can add them to soups, beans, grains, salad dressings, vegetables, sliced cucumbers, potato salad, greens, tomato sauce and stir fry dishes. You can also marinate meat and fish in herbal vinegars or just sprinkle some on the meat while it is cooking or grilling. Just use herbal vinegar in any recipe you would use your ordinary vinegar.

Pineapple Mint Shrub.

Crush fresh Pineapple and mint leaves in a jar. Add the same amount of sugar and apple cider vinegar. Let sit on the bench for up to a week, shaking it when you look at it.

Strain and label. Use this like a cordial.

Citrus vinegar for cleaning.

Add citrus skins to white vinegar as you use them. Let sit on the bench for up to a week, shaking it when you look at it. Strain and label. Dilute with water and use as a spray.

Or just strain off what you need and keep adding the skins and extra vinegar and keep it going.

Rosemary and Lavender Hair Rinse.

Place rosemary and lavender into a jar and cover with apple cider vinegar.
Let sit for at least 2 weeks.
Strain and label.
To use, dilute 1/2 cup of rosemary lavender vinegar with 1 cup water. Apply to hair following a shampooing. Rinse out.

Strawberry Pepper Shrub.

Place 2 teaspoons whole black peppercorns and 1 cup crushed strawberries in a jar.
Add the same amount of sugar and apple cider vinegar. Let sit on the bench for up to a week, shaking it when you look at it.
Strain and label. Use as a cordial or on a salad

Herbal Vinegar Tonic Shrub

Place Nettles, Garlic, Oregano, Marjoram, Rosemary, Chilli (a small amount) into a jar. Add the same amount of sugar and apple cider vinegar. Let sit on the bench for up to a week, shaking it when you look at it. Strain and label. I like 2 teaspoons in a glass of water and as a salad dressing.

Make your own Natural Body Care Products

I am a huge believer in food as medicine. This isn't always just about eating a balanced diet full of vegetables, fruits, nuts, grains, herbs and spices. It's also about what we apply to our skin.

There is so many ways we can help ourselves by creating natural products that have no harsh chemicals or synthetic drugs in them. Creating your own healing balms, creams, lotions and herbal teas and other concoctions like herbal honeys, vinegars, tinctures etc is not just fun, but can be very beneficial.

Drinking herbal teas is a good example. I love to drink a range of herbal teas that calm me down and seem to work well for different issues. For example I will make a cup of Star Anise Tea to drink after dinner because it helps me digest my last meal for the night and gives me a better nights sleep.

Throughout this book and also in my first book "Simple Living, Off the Grid in Oz" I have shared many healthy, healing ideas, like the fermented food and drinks, but I would like to now show you how to create some more products to help you and your family, naturally.

Obviously, if the simple methods aren't enough for you, then please visit your doctor. Also remember to do your own research because sometimes different foods, including herbs can have effects that, if you are pregnant or if you are taking prescribed medications can cause your body to react in ways that aren't good, so check with your doctor if you have any concerns.

Carrier Oils

When making your own natural healing products you will soon find that there are so many options, as far as ingredients go. One of the main ingredients in many products is a carrier oil.

Each Carrier Oils has its own special qualities. I suggest when starting out, that you try using the oils that you have available in your pantry, such as olive oil and coconut oil. Once you have made a few products and enjoy the process, then you can start experimenting with other oils, that may not be available in your local supermarket, but may be available online.

Carrier oils vary in their odour, their shelf life, their absorbability and the way they react to skin types.

Choose the carrier oil that best suits the results you are looking for.

Coconut Oil

It's best to use unrefined coconut oil. Remember that coconut oil often turns to liquid if the temperature is warm, this will effect your product. Fractionated Coconut Oil doesn't harden, so this type can be very useful in different preparations.

Coconut oil has anti fungal, anti bacteria and anti viral qualities.

Coconut oil absorbs quickly into the skin and is a good moisturiser.

Olive Oil

It's best to use Extra Virgin Olive oil. Olive oil can have a strong smell.

Olive oil is a good cleanser for oily skin, and is therefore great in shampoo bars.

It is also a good moisturiser and works well as a massage oil.

Herbal Infused oils are usually made with olive oil.

Sweet Almond Oil

This is a good oil for dry skin and if you are trying to help conditions like psoriasis or eczema as it is very soothing for sore skin.

Avocado Oil

This oil is good moisturising, so it is great for chapped skin.

Avocado oil can also protect skin from sun damage.

Castor Oil

This is a good moisturiser and can help as an anti inflammatory and/or to fight off fungi.

It's good to rub into cuticles to add nourishment,

Some people use this as a laxative.

Apricot Kernel Oil

A good oil to improve skin tone, maintain softness and radiance of the skin. It also nourishes the skin and lowers the appearance of face wrinkles, fine lines and blemishes.

Jojoba Oil

This is not really an oil, but a liquid wax.

Jojoba oil has anti-inflammatory properties which help to tame chaffing and chapping, reduce redness caused by drying, ease the effects of eczema and rosacea, and keep **skin** calm and comfortable. The Vitamin E and B-complex vitamins in the Jojoba oil help in **skin** repair and damage control.

Healing Balms

Creating your own healing balms is quite simple. It's a matter of deciding what you want the end product to do for you, finding the right ingredients that will achieve this and then following the simple process of putting it together.

There are a few rules that you must stick to:

Use clean, dry, dark coloured jars or tins to store them in.

If you are using any ingredient that has water involved, then remember it will not last well. It needs to be refrigerated and used reasonably quickly because it can go rancid and mouldy.

Below is the basic recipe. Add other ingredients such as a vegetable butter, ie shea; infuse the oil with herbs like calendula, comfrey, plantain etc. Use some essential oils which have the effect you are looking for. You can even add in clays, activated charcoal, as I did in the Drawing Salve recipe on page 65. Adding a capsule of vitamin E oil, helps to preserve as does most essential oils.

I could write a whole book on this subject, but I will give you some starting recipes so that you can get a feel for what you are doing and then you can play around and create your own special healing balm,.

Basic Balm Recipe

To every 100gms of oil add 20gms beeswax.

Oils can be whichever one you like or whichever one adds something special to your end product.

Have a look at the carrier oil properties that I have set out for you in the previous pages.

Calendula Salve Recipe

115 grams Calendula Oil
15 grams Beeswax (about 2 tablespoons grated)
25-50 drops Essential Oil, optional
(lavender, frankincense, chamomile and tea tree are good choices)

Melt beeswax with Calendula Oil
Remove from heat and add essential oils.
Blend Well.
Place in clean glass jars.

Sunscreen Bars

1 cup Coconut Oil
1 cup Shea Butter (or Mango, Cocoa or Almond Butter)
1 cup grated Beeswax (or pellets)
2 tablespoon zinc oxide
1 teaspoon Vitamin E Oil

Melt the oil, butter and wax in a glass jar sitting on a chux in some water on the stove.
Add the zinc and stir with a wooden stirrer until well combined.
Add the Vitamin E Oil

Pour into moulds (try paper cake patties)
Allow to set
Store in a glass jar in a cupboard.

Apply as required.

Castor Oil Balm

Castor oil mixed with lanolin is soothing to dry, cracked lips or nipples or heels. It also can be used to smooth and condition eyebrows.

1 teaspoon castor oil
1 teaspoon lanolin or coconut oil
1 teaspoon grated beeswax

Melt castor oil, lanolin and beeswax using a water bath and pour into containers.
Allow to cool completely before placing lid.

Natural Moisturiser

30gm Organic Coconut Oil
2 dessertspoons Jojoba oil
2 dessertspoons Calendula oil
1 teaspoon Rose Petal Glycerite
6 drops Frankincense Essential Oil
6 drops Geranium Essential Oil
6 drops Lavender Essential Oil

Melt the coconut oil with jojoba and Calendula oil.
Remove from heat and add other ingredients and blend well.
Spoon into clean glass jars.

Bath, Shower and Beauty

Making your own personal care items at home is one of my favourite pastimes. They aren't hard to make and you can create products for yourself and for family and friends. Knowing exactly what goes into your products, is especially good, because knowing that they are full of natural ingredients puts your mind at rest. Your body and your pocket will thank you. Once you have the base ingredients in the cupboard you will find that you are saving a lot of money, plus you are making top quality products.

Shampoo

1/4 cup coconut milk (make your own)
1/3 cup liquid castile soap
1/2 teaspoon olive, almond or argon oil
1/2 teaspoon Vitamin E oil
18-20 drops doTERRA essential oil of your choice (My favourite blend is 6 drops each Cedarwood, Lavender and Rosemary)

Combine the ingredients together in a bowl and whisk well.

Apply about 1 tablespoon to scalp and massage in. Rinse and repeat.

Shake it gently before using it.

Herbal Hair Rinse

2 cups boiled Water
3 tablespoons dried Sage
3 tablespoons dried Rosemary
2 tablespoons Apple Cider Vinegar
20 drops Lavender essential oil
20 drops Rosemary essential oil
20 drops Cedarwood essential oil
Infuse the dried herbs in the boiled water until cool. Strain.
Add everything to a bottle and shake.
After shampooing, apply to hair.
Let sit for a couple of minutes and rinse out.

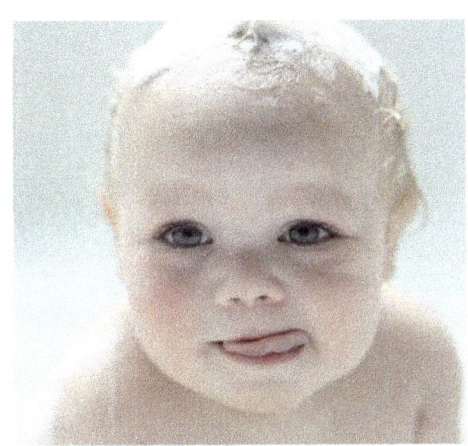

Liquid Baby Shampoo.

1/4 cup Liquid castile soap
1/2 cup Lavender and Chamomile Tea (make this by boiling water and adding 1 teaspoon each lavender and chamomile, let steep until cool. Strain)
1 teaspoon jojoba oil

Add all ingredients to a bowl and gently mix together. Pour into a bottle.

This is also fantastic as a body wash. Very calming.

Honey and Herb Shampoo

1/4 cup coconut milk (make your own)
1/3 cup liquid castile soap
1/2 teaspoon olive, almond or argon oil
1/2 teaspoon Vitamin E oil
1/4 cup Herbal and Honey Tea (make this by boiling water and adding 1 teaspoon each lavender and rosemary. Add the honey and stir to dissolve. Let steep until cool. Strain)

Add all ingredients to a bowl and gently mix together. Pour into a bottle.

Dry Shampoo

So easy to make and take with you. I like this especially when camping and showers aren't easy to come by.

Just mix equal amounts of arrowroot and corn flours together. You can also add cacao powder. When I do this, I use 1 tablespoon each of arrowroot and cornflour and 1 teaspoon of cacao.

Pop it all into a bottle.

Apply it with a make up brush to the scalp. Leave in for a few minutes and then brush it through your hair.

Easy Vapourub

I love this when I have a cold. It is so easy to make.

Store it in a dark glass jar and apply to back and chest.

1/2 cup coconut oil
25 drops Doterra Easy Air Blend or alternatively
10 drops Eucalyptus
10 drops Peppermint

Melt the coconut oil and stir in the essential oils. Pour into jar. Don't apply lid until very cold.

Natural Deodorant

2 tablespoons beeswax pellets (or grated beeswax)
1 tablespoon shea butter
5 tablespoons coconut oil
1/4 cup cornstarch (or arrowroot powder for very sensitive skin)
1/4 cup baking soda
10-15 drops tea tree essential oil
10-15 drops lavender essential oil
10-15 drops of other essential oils
2-3 new or used deodorant tubes (cleaned and twisted all the way back down)

Melt the coconut oil, beeswax and shea butter in a glass jar in a saucepan with water. I like to place a chux under the jar as well.

Mix in the dry ingredients until there are no lumps.

Add the essential oils and stir in well.

Pour into deodorant tubes and allow to cool and set.

Please only use a wooden stirrer when making this recipe.

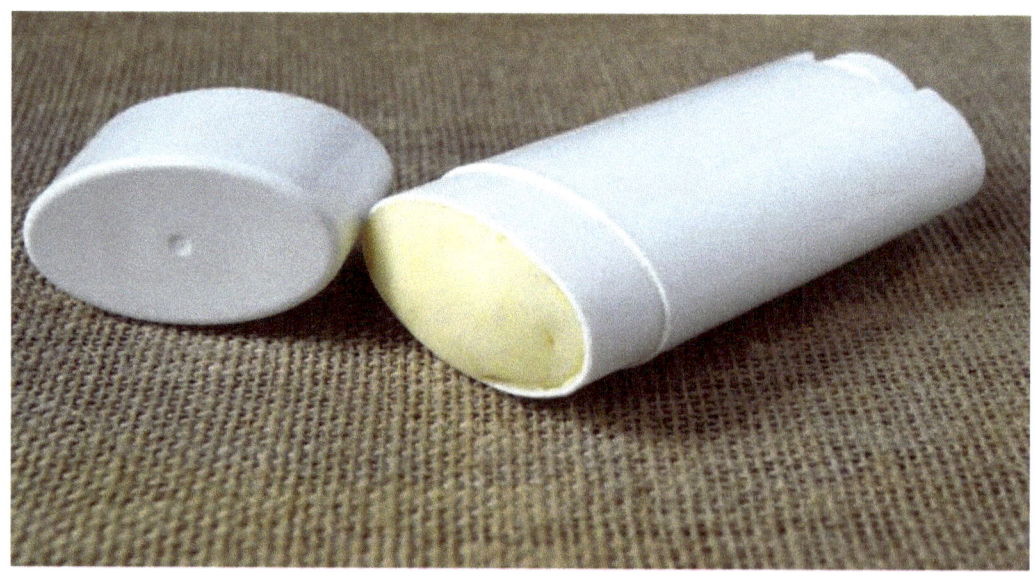

Itchy Skin and Allergy Balm

I like to apply this to midgy and mosquito bites. It also works a treat on hives. If you have allergies to say cats, which I do on occasion, I like to apply this to the sides of my nose and my throat and it helps me breathe easier.

1/4 cup Coconut Oil
1 tablespoon Beeswax (grated or pellets)
15 drops each Lemon, Lavender and Peppermint Essential Oils

Melt the oil and beeswax, in a glass jar which sits on a chux in a saucepan with water.
Add the essential oils and stir with a wooden stirrer

Store in a dark glass cream jar and apply as needed.

After Sun Spray

1/2 cup Witch hazel
2 tablespoons Aloe Vera Gel
10 drops Lavender essential oil
5 drops Tea Tree essential oil
5 drops Chamomile essential oil or peppermint essential oil

Add all the ingredients to a spray bottle and shake to mix.

Apply after coming in from the sun. It may feel a little sticky but just to with that. It's better than feeling crispy.

Bug Repellent Spray

1/2 cup Witch Hazel
8 drops Citronella Essential Oil
8 drops Lemongrass Essential Oil
6 drops Lavender Oil
or... 20 drops Doterra Terra Shield

Place all above into a spray bottle.

Shake well before use.

Lip Balm

2 teaspoons Grated Beeswax (or pellet)
2 teaspoons Olive Oil (or Grapeseed or Sweet Almond Oil)

Melt beeswax and oil together.
Add flavourings then pour into containers.

Get creative with these. Please only use pure essential oils that are safe to be ingested. I only use and recommend Doterra. If you would like to purchase these for yourself please visit my website (mydoterra.com/offthegridinoz)

Mint Chocolate

1 teaspoon Cacao Powder
3 drops Peppermint Essential Oil
Mix this into melted oil and wax thoroughly.

Wild Orange

3-5 drops Wild Orange Essential Oil
Mix this into melted oil and wax thoroughly.

Lime

3-5 drops Lime Essential Oil
Mix this into melted oil and wax thoroughly.

Cinnamon

3 drops Cinnamon Essential Oil
Mix this into melted oil and wax thoroughly.

Lemon Ginger

3 drops Ginger Essential Oil
3 drops Lemongrass or Lemon Essential Oil
Mix this into melted oil and wax thoroughly.

Red Mandarin

3-5 drops Red Mandarin Essential Oil
Mix this into melted oil and wax thoroughly.

Wild Orange

3 drops Wild Orange Essential Oil
Mix this into melted oil and wax thoroughly.

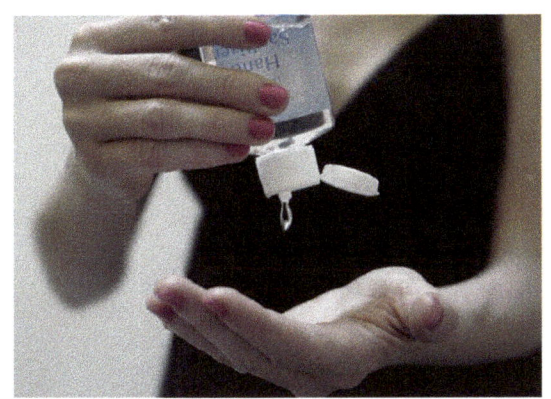

Natural Hand Sanitiser

This is great to have on hand in your hand bag or on the bathroom bench ready for when you need it.

10 drops Lavender Essential Oil
30 drops Tea Tree Essential Oil
OR 40 drops Doterra Onguard Blend (my choice)
1 tablespoon Witch Hazel or Vodka
1/4 teaspoon Vitamin E Oil
3/4 cup Aloe Vera Gel.

Mix the essential oils with the witch hazel and vitamin E oil.
Add Aloe Vera Gel and mix well.

Pour into squirt or pump bottles.

Aromatherapy Bubble Bath

1 cup Liquid Castile Soap
1 cup Filtered water
1/2 cup Vegetable Glycerine
5 Drops Essential Oils of your choice.

Mix all the above together.

Add a few squirts to your bath and relax and enjoy.

Bath Salts

1 cup Magnesium Flakes
1/2 cup Sea or Rock Salt
1/4 cup Baking Soda
10 drops Essential Oils of choice (I like lavender, peppermint, wild orange)
A couple of drops of food colouring if you like.

Mix all together in a jar. You can add dried rose petals or lavender, but I find that a big messy for the clean up. It looks pretty for gifts though.

Moisturising Healing Soap

2 cups Coconut Oil
2 tablespoons Grapeseed Oil (or Olive Oil)
2 tablespoons Liquid Castile Soap
30 drops each Lavender, Lemon and Tea Tree Essential Oils

Whip the coconut oil until smooth.
Add the other ingredients and blend well.
Spoon into a jar that is safe to use in the bathroom.

Sea Salt Body Scrub

1 cup Fine Sea Salt
1/2 cup Grapeseed Oil
1 tablespoon Honey
10 drops Essential Oils (Geranium, Frankincense and Lemon are my choices)

Mix all together and store in a lovely jar.

Massage gently into skin and rinse with warm water.

Ginger Sugar Scrub

1/4 cup Coconut oil
1/4 cup Grapeseed Oil
3/4 cup Sugar
1/4 cup Fine Sea Salt
1 tablespoon grated Ginger

Melt the coconut oil.
Add the grapeseed oil and the ginger.
Leave to infuse over night.
Gently remelt. Strain the ginger out through a coffee filter.
Add the Sugar and Salt and blend with a spoon or fork.
Store in a clean jar.

Massage gently into damp skin. Leave for a couple of minutes. Rinse off with warm water.

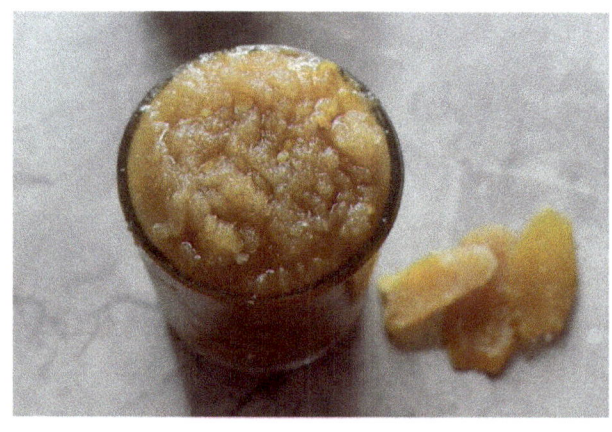

Narnies Recipes

My Grandmother, Narnie's Recipes

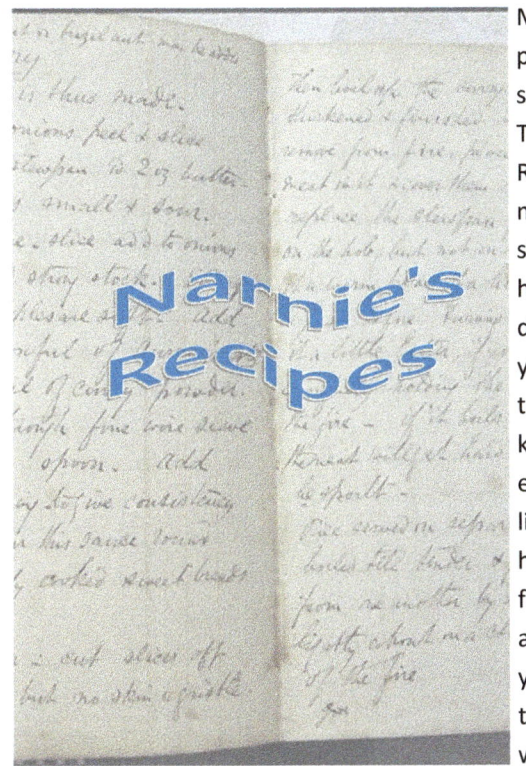

My Grandmother was born in 1904. She was a wonderful person who we called Narnie. Narnie loved to knit, crochet, sew and cook. I have many of her recipes in a file at home. They are hand written and starting to lose their readability. Rather than let them fade into history, I would like to memorialise them here. Many of them are written in a shorthand and I have deciphered as best I could. Although I have included all that was written down, some of these recipes don't tell you everything. For example, they often don't tell you what temperature the oven should be set at or how long to cook for. I imagine this must have been just such common knowledge that it was assumed that it was unnecessary to explain to others. Some of the recipes sound really odd to me, like the Ground Nut Cake. The recipe sounds half finished and I haven't had a chance to try it out. I haven't tried out quite a few of them to be honest, but I hope you enjoy reading them as much as I do and can unravel some of the mysteries for yourself. I have also left the weights and measures authentic to what was written, so you will need to convert them if you would like to try any of them out. Have fun.

I have added some notes here and there to help. Remember these recipes are pre metric, so you will need to convert weights and temperatures.

Golden Syrup Dumplings

2 Cups S.R. Flour
Pinch Salt
1 dessertspoon butter
1 well beaten egg

Mix into light scone dough adding milk or water if necessary.

Bring to boiling point this syrup:

1 Tablespoon butter,
1 cup sugar,
1 cup water,
1 tablespoon Golden Syrup.

Break off small pieces of dumpling drop into syrup.

Put lid on saucepan and simmer 15 minutes.

Christmas Pudding Sauce

1 egg
3/4 cup Caster Sugar
Pinch Salt
1/2 cup cream
3 tablespoons Brandy

Beat egg white
Add sugar and salt
Whisk Egg yoks.
Fold in whipped cream and brandy.

Marinade

3 tablespoons Tomato Sauce
1/2 cup oil
1/4 cup Vinegar
Chopped Onion
Bay Leaf
Salt and Pepper

4 hours or overnight.

Mock Chicken

1 small onion cooked in 1 tablespoon butter. When cooked peel 1 – 2 tomatoes. Cook well. Add dessertspoon grated cheese, salt and pepper and sugar. When cooked add well beaten egg, 1 teaspoon mixed herbs.

(Your guess is as good as mine when it comes to this recipe)

Una's Vanilla Biscuits

1/4 lb butter
1lb sugar
1/2 lb SR Flour
1 egg
1/2 Teaspoon vanilla

Cream butter and sugar. Add beaten egg, flour, vanilla. Drop 1 teaspoon on tray.

Lemon Sago

1 cup Sago
3 cups Water

Soak in water
Add Juice and rind of 3 lemons or 2 lemons and 1 orange
3 tablespoons Golden Syrup
1 Dessertspoon Sugar
Serve with custard

Mother's Biscuits

2 cups SR Flour
1 cup sugar
4 ozs butter
2 eggs

Rub Butter into flour.
Add Sugar and beaten eggs.

Roll out and cut.

Oat Biscuits

4 ozs oats
2 ozs butter
1 oz sugar
Melt butter.
Mix well with oats and sugar.
Press with a knife into a narrow tin.
Cook 45 minutes.
Cut before cold.

Marion's Slices

1/4 Butter
1/2 tin Condensed milk
1 cup cocoanut
1/2 lb coffee biscuits rolled to crumbs
juice and rind of 1 lemon

Mix all together. Roll out, ice. Set in fridge and cut in slices.

Brandied Coffee Delight

2 eggs separated.
1/2 cup sugar
2 tablespoons instant coffee
14 1/2oz can undiluted evaporated milk
1 tablespoon gelatine in 1/4 cup water
2 tablespoons brandy.

Cream egg yolks, sugar and coffee together.
Heat evaporated milk in the top of a double boiler till bubbles appear around the edges.
Stir into the creamed egg yolks gradually
Return to pan and cook stirring till custard thinly coats spoon.
Remove from heat.
Dissolve gelatine and stir into coffee custard.
Cool.
Add brandy and chill till partially set.
Whip the egg whites till very stiff and fold in quickly.
Spoon into a serving bowl or parfait glasses.
Chill till set.
Decorate with whipped coffee or brandy cream and chopped walnuts.
Rum can replace brandy if desired.

Hedgehog

1/2 lb Marie biscuits
3 ozs chopped walnuts
4 ozs butter
4 ozs sugar
2 tablespoons cocoa
1 egg
1 teaspoon vanilla

Crush biscuits. Place in bowl with chopped nuts.
Melt butter, sugar and cocoa in saucepan.
Stir well until blended.
Beat egg, add to chocolate mixture.
Lastly stir in vanilla, mix into broken biscuits.
Mix thoroughly and spread in tin.
Chill overnight. Cut in squares. Ice if desired.

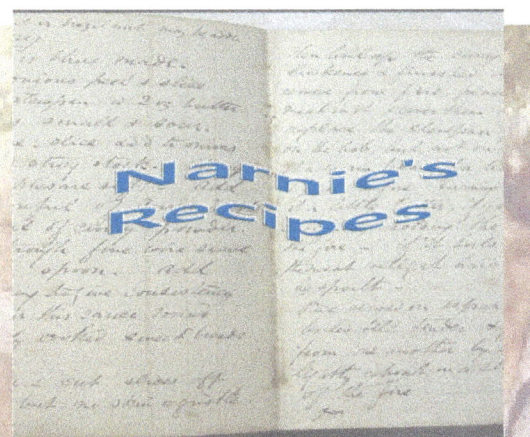

Lucy's Apple Pie

Filling:
5 medium apples, peeled and cored
1/2 cup sugar
1/4 cup water
1/2 teaspoon cinnamon.
Dash of salt.

Slice apples into a medium saucepan.
Add water, sugar, cinnamon and salt
Cook, covered and stirring frequently until water is gone—being careful not to burn apples.
Stir until most lumps are gone.
Turn apples into an 8" pie plate and cover with the following mixture.

Pastry:

1 cup flour
3 tablespoons softened butter
1/2 cup (scant) brown sugar.
Dash cinnamon

Blend ingredients together with fingertips and sprinkle over cooked apples.
Bake in a moderate oven until top is brown and crusty.
Serve warm with whipped cream or vanilla ice cream.

Serves 6 generously.

Chocolate Slice (no egg)

1 1/2 cups SR Flour
1 cup des. Cocoanut
1/2 cup brown sugar
6oz butter

Mix all dry ingredients, melt butter and pour over them.
Mix together and press into swiss roll tin.
Bake 20 mins, till brown.

While still warm ice with peppermint icing:
Sift 6 ozs Icing sugar, Add 1 oz melted copha, 3 dessertspoons milk, 1 teaspoon peppermint essence.

When cold ice with chocolate icing as follows:
Melt 3oz copha and pour it over 1/2 cup drinking chocolate.
Mix well with wooden spoon.
Cool slightly then pour on top of white icing.
Leave to set and cut cake into squares.

Crème de Menthe

1 cup sugar
1/2 cup boiling water
3/4 cup brandy
1 tablespoon gycerine
2 teaspoons peppermint essence
a few drops of green colouring.

Dissolve sugar in water.
When cold mix well with other ingredients.

Ground Nut Cake

3 eggs (separated) (2oz weight)
4 ozs caster sugar.
4 ozs Ground nuts.
Beat whites until stiff.
In another basin beat yolks and sugar until very creamy.
Gradually add egg whites and nuts 1 spoonful at a time.
Note: there is no mention what to do next????

Sylabah

Juice 1 lemon
2oz Caster sugar
1/2 pint cream
Beat all together.

Put a little rum in each dish then mixture then rum on top. Uses about 1 wine glass rum

Pineapple & Orange

Tin Evaporated milk
Packet Lemon Jelly
3/4 cup Pineapple juice
3/4 cup orange juice
1/2 cup sugar.

Put juice and sugar to heat then add jelly. Stir and put in bowl to set.
Whip chilled milk and add.
Cover with crushed chocolate biscuits (about 8-10)
Top with whipped cream.

Marshmallow Dessert

1/2 cup orange juice add 1 tablespoon gelatine and 1 teaspoon vanilla. Fill cup with hot water. Beat 3 egg whites stiffly, add gradually 3/4 cup sugar, then cool juice mixture. Beat all well together. Put in greased tin.

Rum Mousse

1 tin evaporated milk
3 teaspoons gelatine
1/2 cup hot water
2 teaspoons instant coffee
1/2 dup caster sugar
2 tablespoons Rum

Whip milk in a large bowl
Add sugar.
Dissolve gelatine in hot water. Cool.
Add to milk with coffee and rum.

Pavlova

1 egg white
Pinch Salt
3/4 cup Caster Sugar
1 teaspoon vinegar
1 teaspoon cornflour
2 tablespoons boiling water.
Beat all together

300* 1 1/4 hours

Choc Rolls

1/2 lb crushed sweet biscuit crumbs
1/2 cup cocoanut
2 tablespoons cocoa
1 tin condensed milk

Place all ingredients in bowl and combine. Form into small log shapes and roll in extra cocoanut and allow to set firm—no cooking required.

Lemon Slice

1 packet Marie biscuits
add 1 cup coconut
Grate 2 lemons and mix into 1/4 lb melted butter. Stir in well with 1/2 can condensed milk.

Icing: Squeeze 2 lemons and add to sifted icing sugar before freezing.

Cinnamon Cheese Pie

Crush 3 tablespoons melted butter, 1 tablespoon sugar, 1 cup biscuit crumbs, 1/2 cup chopped walnuts, 1/2 teaspoon cinnamon and nutmeg.

Filling: 8 oz cream cheese, 1/2 cup condensed milk, 2 tablespoons lemon juice, 1/2 cup whipped cream.
Mix all pie crust ingredients together. Press into a 9" pie dish. Chill while preparing filling.

Beat cream cheese, add milk, lemon juice and beat till smooth. Fold in whipped cream. Pour into pie crust. Chill 3 hours. Decorate top with cinnamon. Serve with whipped cream.

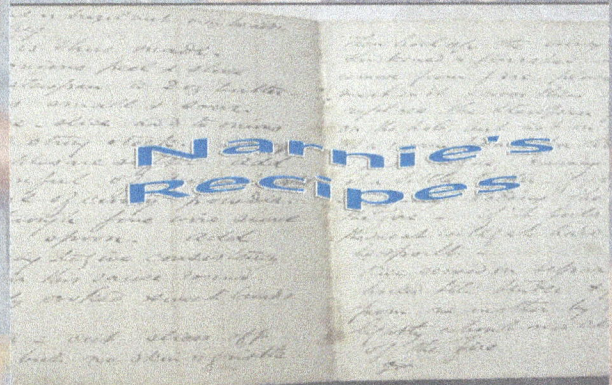

Apricot Cream Pie

one 8" shortbread pastry case. 14 1/2 oz can evaporated milk, chilled icy cold. I packet vanilla instant pudding, 1 large can apricots, 2 tablespoons apricot jam. Place tin milk in bowl, sprinkle instant pudding on the ilk and beat 30 –60 seconds until well mixed. Place in pastry case. Leave to set. Drain apricots and arrange on set instant pudding. Heat jam gently. Rub through a sieve. Spoon over apricots. Place in fridge to chill.

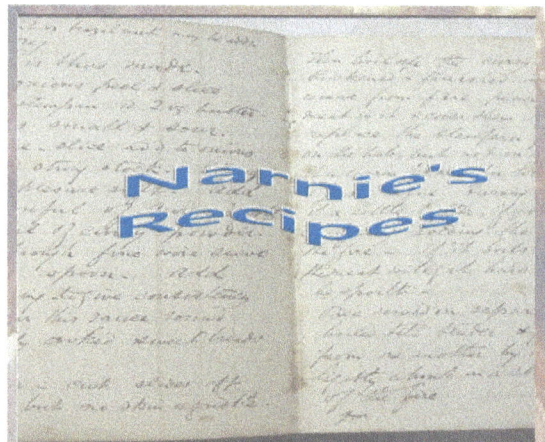

Strawberry Shortcake

4 oz butter
4 oz Castor sugar,
4 oz SR flour
2 oz cornflour
2 eggs

Cream the butter and sugar until light and soft then sift the flour and cornflour. Add beaten eggs to creamed butter and fold in the flour with a metal spoon.

Place the mixture in tins and flatten on top, baking for 20 minutes at 375 to400 degrees until crisp and golden brown.

The filling is a small punnet of fresh strawberries, a quarter of a pint of thick cream, one egg white and sugar.

Whip the cream in one bowl and the egg white in another then fold together, sweetening to taste.

Cover one shortcake with some of the strawberries and cream and top with second shortcake and rest of cream and fruit.

Use two, seven inch lined sandwich tins for cooking.

Coffee Biscuit

3 oz butter
1 tablespoon sugar
1 tablespoon golden syrup
1 teaspoon instant coffee
8 oz plain sweet biscuits crumbs
3 oz dark cooking chocolate

Cream butter and sugar. Add golden syrup and coffee and mix in crumbs. Pack into a greased 8 in square tin. Press down well. Melt chocolate in basin over hot water. Pour over biscuit mixture, spreading evenly with a knife. Leave to set for 3 hours in the refrigerator then cut into squares.

Lemon Delicious

2 oz SR Flour
1 oz butter
4 oz sugar
2 lemons
2 eggs separated
1 1/4 pints milk

Sift flour, cream butter and sugar. Add sifted flour and mix well. Add grated rind of 1 lemon and juice of two. Add beaten egg yolks and milk. Fold in stiffly beaten egg whites. Pour into greased pie dish. Stand in dish of hot water and bake in oven at 400degrees for 10 minutes. Reset to 350 degrees for about 1/2 hour. When cooked it should be firm on top with a creamy custard underneath.

Sauted Beef

2 lbs bladebone steak	1/2 cup white wine	butter
1 tbsp oil	2 tsp tomato paste	mushrooms
1 tbsp butter	1 1/4 cups good jellied stock	stale bread
1 small onion	1 clove garlic	oil for frying
2 tbsp flour (more flour may be added if a thicker sauce wanted)		parsley

Cut the meat into 1 inch squares. Heat the oil in a pan, add the butter and when foaming ad the meat, and lightly brown on all sides. Remove and keep warm.

Reduce the heat and add the finely chopped onion, and cook slowly until just taking colour. Stir in the flour, and continue cooking to a russet brown. Draw aside, blend in the wine, tomato paste, stock bouquet garni and the garlic, crushed with the salt.

Replace the meat, stir until boiling, cover and cook gently for about 1 1/4 hours or until the meat is tender. About 15 minutes before the meat is cooked, add the quartered mushrooms.

Cut six triangular shaped croutes from the bread and fry in hot oil until golden brown. Drain and set aside.

When the meat is tender, serve. Reduce the remaining sauce by boiling rapidly util of the consistency desired. Spoon the sauce over the meat and surround with the croutes. Dust with parsley and serve with potato puree, glazed carrots and broccoli.

Potato Puree:

Peel the potatoes and put into a pan. Cover with cold water, ad salt and bring slowly to the boil. Cook until tender, and then strain; return to the pan and dry over the heat for a few moments.

Rub through a fine wire sieve, add a little butter, sat and pepper, level the surface of the potato puree, and pour over a "lid" of hot milk. (NOTE: A lid is enough hot milk to cover the surface of the potato to achieve a creamy consistency when later beaten through) When ready to serve, beat well.

Glazed Carrots

1 lb carrots	1 tbsp sugar
knob butter	2 1/4 cups water
pinch salt	Chopped Parsley

Scrape the carrots and cut into 1 1/2" matchstick shapes. Melt the sugar and the butter in a saucepan, add the carrots, water and salt. Bring to the boil and simmer for 15 minutes or until the carrots are cooked.

Remove the carrots. Boil the liquid until reduced to one-third of the original quantity. Return to the pan an stir gently to glaze all over. Serve sprinkled with coarsely chopped parsley.

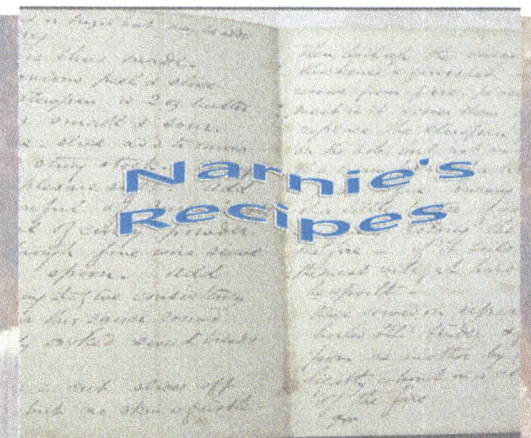

Narnie's Recipes

This recipe didn't have a name?

4 handfuls of oats
1 onion
1/4 lb suet

Mix the minced onion and chopped suet with meat add salt and pepper and moisten with water. Mix well again and tie into a scalded and floured cloth. Boil for 2 hours.

NOTE: I would assume the meat is minced?

Savoury Lamb Chops (another recipe)

2 tablespoons flour
1 tablespoon sugar
1/4 teaspoon each: ground ginger, mustard curry spice.
2 tablespoons vinegar
Chopped parsley
2 tablespoons tomato sauce
1 cup water stock or gravy

Trim chops. Place in buttered casserole. Pour mixture over an leave 1 hour.

Bake 2 hours in slow oven

Creamy Celery Soup

1 cup chopped, cooked celery
1/2 cup chopped cooked onion or leeks
2 tablespoons flour
1 cup milk
1 teaspoon salt
dash cayenne pepper

Mash vegetables or put through sieve, then add flour, salt and pepper and stir. Add milk, stir and heat gently until thickened. Do not boil. Stir in knob of butter and sprinkle with fine chopped parsley.

Pavlova

Four egg whites, a good pinch of salt and a good pinch of cream of tartar, one and half cups sugar, one slightly rounded dessertspoon cornflour, one teaspoon vinegar, on teaspoon vanilla.

Place the egg whites in a warm, dry basin. Add the salt and the cream of tartar and beat until the egg whites will hold their shape. Now ad half the sugar, a little at a time, beating well after each addition.

The mixture should be thick and glossy, Quickly fold in the remaining sugar, sifted cornflour, then the vinegar and vanilla. Place the pavlova into a prepared tin, or on the back of an oven tray which has been well greased, and bake in a slow oven, temp. 300 deg, for one and a quarter hours.

Cheese Squares

Good way to use up left over porridge. Reheat porridge and while still hot, stir in a good dessertspoon of dripping. Add 2 or 3 dessertspoons of grated cheese for every 2 cups of porridge. Add salt and pepper. Stir until cheese is melted. Pour into shallow dish. When cold and firm, cut into squares. Flour both sides and fry until crisp in very hot fat.

Savoury Lamb Chops

1 barbecue cut lamb chop per person
1 packet French onion soup mix
1 can tomato soup

Place chops in pan and sprinkle French onion soup mix over top then pour tomato soup over. Cover pan with foil and bake in a moderate oven for about an hour.

Jacks

3 cups oats
3 oz butter
3 oz brown sugar
1/2 teaspoon baking powder

Knead all together using some flour to stop sticking. Roll out and cut with a cutter into small biscuits. Bake in a moderate oven for about 10 minutes. Let cool on tin.

Savoury Sauce

1/2 oz cayenne, 1/2 oz garlic, 1 quart white vinegar, 1 gill soy. Using a mortar pound the garlic and cayenne well. Add vinegar gradually. When well mixed, strain through a hair sieve. Add soy and bottle.

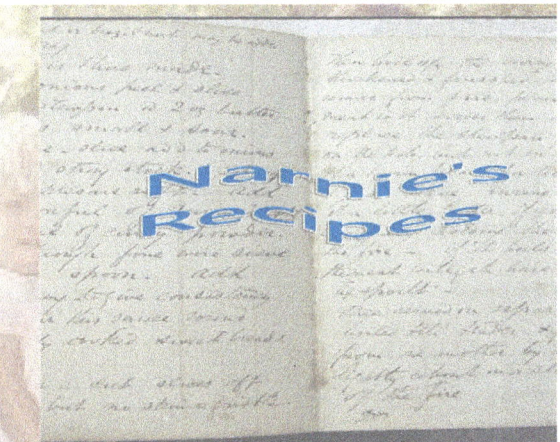

Baked Savoury Pudding.

Heap a pint basin with small pieces of stale bread, soak in a little cool water, then squeeze as dry as possible. Beat with a fork. Boil 2 large onions for 10 minutes and dice. Mix with the bread, add 4 tablespoons of finely chopped suet, 2 good tablespoons of fine oatmeal, a teaspoon of powdered sage, a little marjoram, salt and pepper to taste and 3 eggs. Spread into a greased Yorkshire pudding tin about 3/4 of an inch thick. Bake for about an hour in a moderate oven. The top will be brown and the sides slightly crisp. Serve with gravy.

Tomato Sauce

2 dozen tomatoes, 1/2 oz salt, 1 lemon
1 oz minced onions, 1 pint vinegar, 6 capsicums
1/2 oz white pepper.

Stalk and wipe and then put the tomatoes in a jar in the oven. Leave them all night. Rub them through a sieve and weigh the pulp. To each 2lb of pulp take the proportion of ingredients above. Boil the vinegar and other ingredients 8 to 10 minutes then mix with the tomato pulp, and the strained lemon juice. Put all into a pan and heat over a gentle fire until it becomes the consistency of cream. Put into dry wide mouthed jars, when cold, cork securely.

Index

After Sun Spray (117)

Air Freshener (90, 103)

All Purpose Cleaner (90)

Almond Milk (72)

Anti Inflammatory Kombucha Tonic (49)

Apple and Ginger Fermented Honey (65)

Apple Cider Vinegar (41)

Apple Cider Vinegar Body Scrub (44)

Apple Cider Vinegar Detox Bath (44)

Apple Cider Vinegar Facial Toner (43)

Apple Cider Vinegar Fruit and Vege Scrub (44)

Apple Cider Vinegar Shrub (46)

Apple Sourdough Pancakes (19)

Apricot Cream Pie (127)

Apricot Kernel Oil (111)

Aromatherapy Bubble Bath (119)

Avocado Oil (111)

Baked Savoury Pudding (131)

Basic Balm Recipe (112)

Basic Bread Recipe (9)

Bath Salts (119)

Bath, Shower and Beauty (114)

Beat Seasonal Allergies with Honey (59)

Beeswax (66)

Beeswax Modelling Clay (68)

Beeswax Sticks (69)

Beeswax Wraps (67)

Berry Fermented Honey (65)

Berry Lemonade (52)

Blood Shrub (47)

Body Care Products (109)

Brandied Coffee Delight (125)

Bread Making (7)

Brining (29)

Bug Repellent Spray (117)

Calendula Oil (101)

Calendula Salve (112)

Cardiovascular Shrub (47)

Carrier Oils (110)

Cashew, Avocado and Kefir Dip (38)

Castor Oil (111)

Castor Oil Balm (113)

Cheese Squares (131)

Cheese Waxing (66)

Choc Rolls (127)

Chocolate Sourdough Muffins (20)

Chocolate Blueberry and Kefir Muffins (39)

Chocolate Slice (No Egg) (126)

Christmas Pudding Sauce (123)

Cinnamon Cheese Pie (127)

Citrus Lemonade (52)

Citrus Shrub (46)

Citrus Vinegar (91, 108)

Coconut Cream (73)

Coconut Milk (73)

Coconut Oil (110)

Coffee Biscuits (128)

Comfrey Oil (101)

Cornflour Cleaning (94)

Cough and Sore Throat Reliever (59)

Creamy Celery Soup (130)

Crème de Menthe (126)

Cucumber Kefir Face Mask (38)

Diffusing (104)

Dishwasher Tablets (91)

Disinfectant (90)

Dog Bed Spray (104)

Drawing Salve (69)

Dry Shampoo (115)

Easy Scrolls (23)

Easy Vapourub (116)

English Muffins (21)

Exotic Marshmallows (104)

Face Mask (106)

Face Mist (103)

Fermented Drinks (45)

Fermented Fruit Leather (32)

Fermented Garlic Honey (64)

Fermented Honey Garlic Vinaigrette (64)

Fermenting (26)

Fermenting Foods (28)

Fermenting Fruit (32)

Fizzy Herbal Tea (51)

Flat Bread (22)

Flavouring Kombucha (49)

Floor Cleaners (93)

Fluffy Rice (44)

Focus Spray (104)

From Ferments to Alcohol (33)

Fruit Fly Trap (44)

Furniture Polish (90)

Garlic Aioli (82)

Geranium Moisturiser (106)

Ginger Bug (50)

Ginger Lemon (54)

Ginger Sugar Scrub (120)

Golden Syrup (81)

Golden Syrup Dumplings (123)

Gnocchi (24)

Grease Biscuit Trays (66)

Ground Nut Cake (126)

Hair Rinse (106)

Healing Balms (112)

Healthy Chocolate Milk (76)

Healthy Lemonades (50)

Hedgehog (125)

Herbal English Muffins (22)

Herb and Cheese Sweet Potato Muffins (24)

Herbal Hair Rinse (114)

Herbal Honey Lozenges (61)

Herbal Honey Pills (61)

Herbal Infused Oils (99)

Herbal Infused Vinegars (107)

Herbal Vinegar Tonic Shrub (108)

Herbs and Natural Products (98)

Home Made Nutella (76)

Home Made Substitutions (cleaning) (88)

Honey (56)

Honey and ACV Hair Rinse (60)

Honey and Herb Shampoo (115)

Honey Fermentation (63)

Honey Hair Mask (60)

Honey in the Garden (62)

Household firelighters (95)

Hydrosol (102)

Itchy Skin & Allergy Balm (117)

Jacks (131)

Jojoba Oil (111)

Keep Calm (104)

Kefir (37)

Kefir Cheese (40)

Kefir Lemonade (40)

Kefir Scones (39)

Kefir Sauerkraut (38)

Kimchi (30)

Kimchi Fried Rice (31)

Kimchi Fitters or Pancakes (31)

Kombucha (48)

Labneh (35)

Labneh Mousse (36)

Laundry Detergent (89)

Leather Polish (66)

Lemon Delicious (128)

Lemon, Lime and Blueberry (54)

Lemon and Passionfruit Lemonade (51)

Lemon Pepper Seasoning (82)

Lemon Sago (124)

Lemon Slice (127)

Linen Spray (104)

Lip Balm (118)

Liquid Baby Shampoo (115)

Lucy's Apple Pie (125)

Make Flour from the pulp (74)

Make These from Scratch too. (80)

Make your own Hydrosol (102)

Mango and Banana Smoothie (40)

Mango Labneh Spread (36)

Marinade (124)

Marinated Labneh Balls (35)

Marion's Slice (124)

Marshmallow Dessert (126)

Mashed Potato Muffins (24)

Mayonnaise (81)

Milk Kefir (37)

Mixed Berry Shrub (46)

Mock Chicken (124)

Moisturising Healing Soap (120)

Mosquito Repellent (103)

Mother's Biscuits (124)

- Narnies Recipes (122)
- Natural Cockroach Help (89)
- Natural Deodorant (116)
- Natural Hand Sanitiser (119)
- Natural Household Cleaning (86)
- Natural Moisturiser (113)
- No Knead Modern Bread (12)
- Non Scratch Scouring Powder (91)
- Nut Butter (74)
- Nut Milk (72)
- Nut Milk Ice Cream (75)
- Nuts and Milks (71)
- Oat Biscuits (124)
- Olive Oil (110)
- Oven Cleaner (90)
- Pasties (23)
- Pavlova (127, 130)
- Peach and Cinnamon Honey (65)
- Pineapple and Orange (126)
- Pineapple Kombucha (49)
- Pineapple Mint Shrub (108)
- Pistachio Nut Cheese (77)
- Pizza Base Easy (22)
- Pizza Dough (14)
- Plum Honey (54)
- Plum Shrub (46)
- Post Workout Recovery (44)
- Prevent Rust (66)
- Rice Milk (73)
- Roasted Nut Milk (74)
- Rock Cakes (23)
- Room Spray (106)
- Rose Honey (54)
- Rose Jelly (103)
- Rosemary Oil (101)
- Rosemary and Lavender Hair Rinse (108)
- Rum Mousse (127)
- Salad Dressing (43, 105)
- Sauted Beef (129)
- Savoury Lamb Chops (130, 131)
- Savoury Sauce (131)
- Sea Salt Body Scrub (120)
- Shampoo (114)
- Shoe Deodoriser (91)
- Shrub Remedies (47)
- Sleeping Aid (59)
- Sourdough Bread (15)
- Stay Cool (104)
- Starting from Scratch (5)
- Strawberry Mint Kefir (54)
- Strawberry Pepper Shrub (108)
- Strawberry Shortcake (128)
- Sunflower Milk (73)
- Sunscreen Bars (113)
- Super White Powder (84)

Sweet Almond Oil (111)

Sweet Chilli Dip (36)

Sweetened Condensed Milk (81)

Sweet Muffins (22)

Sweet Potato Muffins (24)

Sweet Rose Labneh (35)

Sylabah (126)

Tartare Sauce (82)

Toilet Bowl Cleaner (92)

Tomato Sauce (131)

Traditional Bread (9)

Tub & Tile Cleaners (92)

Tzatziki (83)

Una's Vanilla Biscuits (124)

Washing Powder (89)

Water Kefir (53)

Waterproof Shoes and Boots (66)

What makes a Simple Life (4)

Window Cleaner (91)

Wood Furniture Polish (92)

Wood Lubricant (66)

Worcestershire Sauce (83)

Wound care (59)

Yoghurt (34)

Yummo Magnesium Rich Balls (78)

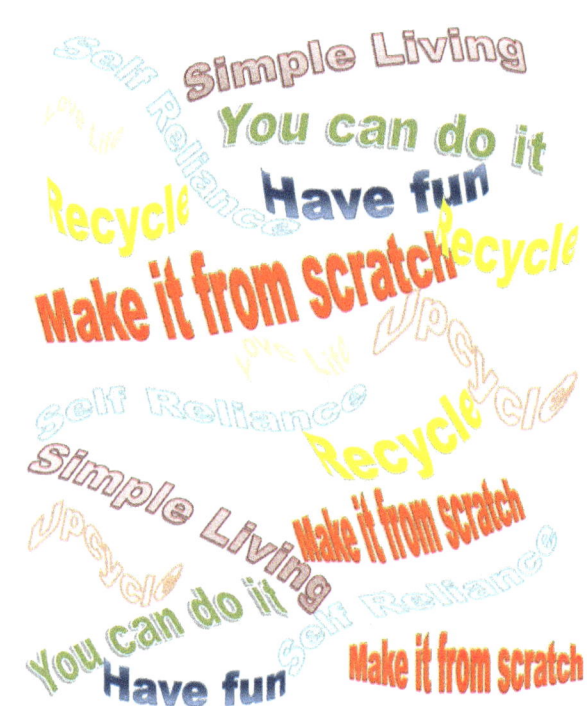

The Last Word

I really hope that you have enjoyed this book.

Don't forget that I have another book called "Simply Living, Off the Grid in Oz" that tells all about how we live off the grid in Australia. It includes everything that you will need to know about harvesting, storing and maintaining solar, water and vegetable growing using hydroponics, wicker beds and guerrilla buckets. There is also so many, hints, tips and recipes to get you motivated in making your own products and meals. Plus a whole lot more.

If you would like a copy of "Simple Living, Off the Grid in Oz" contact me. I'm happy to autograph every book I sell personally, or of course you can purchase it from a whole range of online stores.

If you need to contact me, you can write to my email kezzeens@gmail.com or you can find me on Facebook

https://www.facebook.com/simplelivingoffthegridinoz or do a search for Kerri-Ann Price.

I really do hope that you are feeling like starting your journey to a more simpler, more creative life, Starting from Scratch.

Cheers Kerri.

PS: We have a YouTube channel with a whole heap of our videos free to watch. Put in a search for Off the Grid in Oz.

And don't forget about our website: http://offthegridinoz.com

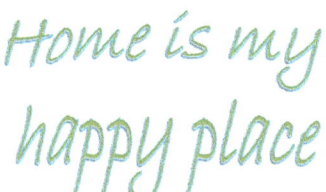

Disclaimer: I am not trained in any medical or chemical or cosmetic field. I am a sharer of what I have tried and love. Please do your own research if you have any concerns. A good idea, when trying out new things on your skin, is to do a little patch test to see if you have any reaction. If you do, then perhaps try a different product. I can't take any responsibility for what you do with my ideas.

www.ingramcontent.com/pod-product-compliance
Lightning Source LLC
Chambersburg PA
CBHW061133010526
44107CB00068B/2927